THE INFLUENCE OF CHRISTIANITY ON EARLY TEXAS HISTORY

By Dr. Bill Miller

MAKE A WAY PUBLISHING
Granbury, Texas

Make a Way® Ministries inc

The Influence of Christianity on Early Texas History
© January 2014 by Dr. William Miller

MAKE A WAY® PUBLISHING
AKA Cornerstone Financial Counselors
Granbury, Texas

To contact MAKE A WAY® MINISTRIES INC:

Operating Office:
P.O. Box 1164
Granbury, Texas 76048

Corporate Office:
12030 SW 129 Court
Suite 104
Miami, Florida 33186

(800) 357-4223

www.makeawaypublishing.com
www.makeaway.net
www.creditcounseling.net

Face Book:
Make A Way Ministries
Granbury Financial Freedom

ISBN-10: 0970080344
ISBN-13:978-0-9700803-4-9

Foreword

TEXAS! Just the sound of that word stirs something within those of us who are Texans. Non-Texans say it's due to ego and pride—if that's the case, then why don't they feel the same way about their state? No, there is something about this great state that historians have tried to put their finger on for as long as anyone can remember. And it seems that more books, papers and articles have been written about Texas than some libraries can hold.

Dr. Bill Miller has undertaken a study that has long been overlooked and in this day and time, many want to ignore or reject. The basis of his writing is the truth that Almighty God has been involved in the development and spirit of this land more than some are willing to admit. He shows evidence of behind-the-scenes events that began long before Texas was discovered by Europeans, which can only be attributed to the Hand of God!

As he points out, this volume is not merely another history book. But it is intended to acknowledge the many ways that the Lord has directed the course of events in order to bring the Gospel of Jesus Christ to the New World. Readers will find his presentation very interesting and worthwhile. It will also enhance the healthy form of pride in being a part of something much larger than any of us may have even imagined.

May the Lord bless you as you take the time to discover the greatness of Texas, from this perspective, but even more may you recognize the glory and honor due to Almighty God for blessing this great state!

Pastor Glenn Ward
Director of Missions
Paluxy Baptist Association
Granbury, Texas

Dedication

This little book is dedicated to the people who love Texas and want to be a part of what God is still doing here with special regard for the *Texas Heroes Foundation* in Granbury, Texas

Contents

Introduction

When people typically consider Texas history, they don't usually give much thought to the fact that the Church of Jesus Christ played a key role in its unfolding. Things didn't just happen here by accident like a random series of events that somehow worked together to produce the place and the culture we so enjoy all these years later. Rather, God's hand was on this place a long time ago because the geographic area we now call Texas was right in the exact path of His plan to spread Christianity all around the globe. What God promised Abraham way back in Genesis 12:3 came right through Texas:

"...And in you all the families of the earth will be blessed."

And so, this is a little book that has been written to highlight how the Church has helped shape and determine our history. It was written as a series of articles and I'm not exactly sure why I did it that way. Put them all together and they make a small book with just enough space to bring out some highlights and not enough to go into a lot of religious and historical detail. And by the way, I made the arbitrary decision for "early history" in this book to end in 1899 at the end of the nineteenth century. If what you read makes you hungry for more, by all means go out on the Internet and search for it because there's a wealth of information out there about the history of our state.

The truth is I am an ordained minister and not a historian although I come from a family of historians. What that means is that I get real excited when I discover that God's hand has been on something, subtly and quietly directing things when nobody was paying much attention. Those discoveries are special "ah-ha" moments that make me want to write some articles or a book so others can "ah-ha" too. On the other hand, if you were looking for some deep intellectual study of history when you bought this book, you should go get your money back because I didn't write it that way and wouldn't know how to anyway.

In sum, this isn't a history book that delves into the depth of historical detail that history buffs are so fond of. Most of that has been omitted by intent. Rather the purpose has been to show how the plan of God to bring the Gospel of the Kingdom to the New World was accomplished through the Christian religion of those times and how that worked to shape the destiny of Texas by interacting with some of the major secular activities of the day that were going on at the same time. The Body of Christ doesn't work perfectly so the shaping of our destiny hasn't been a perfect work. But it has produced one of the most unique places on earth where Christians get things done together in a hybrid confluence of ethnic cultures united in the cause of Christ.

For what it's worth, I was born in Houston, Texas quite a while ago, grew up in Dallas and attended Texas Tech University in Lubbock. It took me a long time to get out of that place and start my career, so I know Texas deeply, down in my heart. Over my adult life though, I've lived and traveled all around our country and all around Latin America. I speak Spanish and have an insightful understanding of the Hispanic culture. I love the people and I love their influence on the history and unique culture of Texas. And because of having to travel so much over the years I can tell you this from experience: of all the places I have ever visited or lived, Texas is the one place that far and away looks back on its history with the most interest and reverence and gratitude and pride. And friend, it is really something special.

Thank you for purchasing this little book. Proceeds are being used to fund Christian ministerial projects mostly in Texas so you have sown seed into good ground. I hope you enjoy this fresh perspective on history and have some fun with it. May God bless you and your family in every area of life!

Dr. Bill Miller
May 2014

Part One:
The Indians

This is a series of articles highlighting the influence of Christianity on the unique history and culture of Texas. The truth is the current character of a people has been significantly influenced by its religious history. And Texas is certainly no exception even though when we usually talk about our particularly rich history of independence and cowboys and cattle and individualism and gun slingers and strong pioneering people and oil wells and all the rest of it, our tendency is to <u>not</u> focus all that much on the part that has come about because of the design and providence of God.

All nations and peoples of the world for all of history have at various times been raised up and set down by God as part of an overall, long-term, divinely-inspired plan to expand His Kingdom over the entire earth. The development of Texas isn't an accident or the result of a series of random coincidences that somehow finally coalesced into what we've become. No, history has brought us to this place and at this time as part of a master plan, and God's hand in that process is clearly revealed by looking more closely at how Christianity has been intimately involved in it all along the way.

Also, when most people start thinking about Texas history, we just naturally take up with it a little before the *Alamo* and the struggle for independence, and after that we became a republic for a time, and after that we were annexed into the U.S. and wound up on the Confederate side of the Civil War. That much is a wonderful history to be remembered and celebrated. But before any of that happened, there were more than five thousand years of history here in Texas that most folks are a little fuzzy on.

Before Europeans "discovered" this place there had been "Indians" wandering around through here for thousands of years. Some of them didn't take too kindly to the idea of new folks moving into the area and they made things difficult for a while. Where did they come from and when did they get here? What had they been doing all that time? The truth again is God had a lot to do with that story, and it seemed right to start at the very beginning of it and find out what happened back there before all the regular history we're more familiar with came along.

The Plan of God

God always has a plan for everything. He doesn't do anything or say anything without a purpose behind it. And pursuing a purpose always requires a plan for eventually achieving it. According to the Bible the main purpose of God has always been to establish (expand) His Kingdom over the entire earth. When I say that God has a *plan* for that process, I need to put it in the proper context because there's a lot of secular thinking about the history of the earth and of mankind that directly contradicts the Bible. Personally, I like to always agree with the Bible and it says that the earth is approximately 6,000 years old, that God created it in six days by SPEAKING it into existence and that human life started on the sixth day in a place called The *Garden of Eden* located in the vicinity of present day Iraq. All that is described in quite a bit of detail in the first two chapters of the Book of Genesis.

Included there is the historical documentation confirming that God mandated and empowered His first two human beings to subdue and eventually rule over everything on the entire earth (Genesis 1:28). In other words, they were to start from that Garden and work under the authority of the mandate they had been given until they had expanded the Kingdom of God everywhere. I don't know why God wanted to do it that way; He just did and He set up a specific plan for it even though He had given a free will to those folks and knew ahead of time that they would soon use it in a way that would make it necessary for that original plan to be repeatedly modified even though it had been PERFECTLY designed.

Those modifications included, among other things, a worldwide flood approximately 4,500 years ago that wiped out all life on the earth with just a very few exceptions. The reason God did that was because those first folks just had not been willing to pursue His purpose for the earth so He judged them. According to the biblical account, the Prophet Noah built a giant boat according to God's specifications so there could be a place of refuge during the time the earth was under water. The only occupants of that boat were Noah and his wife plus their three sons and their wives, a total of eight people, plus numerous pairs of animals and plants so that life could be restored to the earth after the Flood.

Every living thing left on the earth that was not on that boat perished in the Flood. And if you have problems believing the biblical account of this event, it might help you to know that the geological evidence now confirms that there was indeed a worldwide flood. The only significant difference of opinion is over when it occurred. The Bible says it was about 4,500 years ago, the evolutionists and their group don't really know when it happened but by their measure it had to have been millions of years ago. As I've already said, I always go with what the Bible says about everything and that includes the worldwide flood.

It didn't take long for the descendants of Noah's family to get things messed up again and less than three hundred years after the flood had subsided God needed to make another major modification of His plan. Modifications don't really bother God because whatever He does works out right no matter how much human imperfection He has to deal with. This time, all those descendants had gotten together and decided to build the *Tower of Babel* in about the year 2240 BC instead of going out to pursue God's main purpose of expanding His Kingdom: same God, same purpose. So to carry out this plan modification, God scattered mankind abroad over the face of the whole earth (Genesis 11:8).

The Scattering

In time, that *Scattering* reached the New World and people came to North America and to Texas and all over the New World including some islands in the Caribbean Ocean that Columbus came to in 1492 A.D. From the time of *The Scattering* from Babel until Columbus arrived in the New World, more than 3,700 years passed and a lot of people and their descendants had found their way to the Americas all the way from Alaska and the north of Canada down through the U.S. to Mexico to Central America and the Caribbean Basin and eventually down to almost the southern tip of South America.

But how did they get here? And where did they come from? The Bible-based answers to those questions are really thought provoking. The place called *Babel* where *The Scattering* started from was in Babylon, once again in what is now Iraq in the region called the Middle East. Even three centuries after the Flood it is thought that all the continents were still bound together. But about the same time that *The Scattering* was starting, the continents began to separate because of stress caused by the Flood and climate change which was also caused by the Flood. The people had been supernaturally motivated to *scatter* so they began to move quickly to the destinations all over the earth that God had planned for them.

It's also thought that the first post-flood people to come to North America crossed by a land bridge over what is now the Behring Strait between Alaska and Russia. OR, it's also possible that they came over just before the continents began to split apart. About that same time an Ice Age started in the far North because of that same flood-caused climate change. It lasted for several centuries and served to drive the people southward. Look then at how God's plan is working: the people are supernaturally motivated to *scatter*, they come to North America, the continents split apart and the land connection they came over on disappears so they can't go back to where they came from. And an Ice Age starts so that most of them will keep moving and go south until they populate all of the New World, almost all the way down to Antarctica.

And by the way, many of the animals including a number of the dinosaur types came along with them right on into Texas. There are fossils all over our state that corroborate this and they were laid down AFTER the flood. There's also a multitude of wonderful cave drawings that are known by the geological evidence to have been drawn AFTER the flood and they confirm that the dinosaurs and mammoths and people were contemporaneous inhabitants of North America. Near Glen Rose, Texas for example you can find some of that fossil evidence along with the *Creation Evidence Museum* where you can learn about all the physical evidence that confirms the Bible's account of how the earth became populated after the great Flood.

Now to be consistent with biblical accounts, *The Scattering* and the almost simultaneous splitting apart of the continents would have occurred somewhere between 2200 and 2100 B.C. Of course what I'm proposing here will pretty much drive secular anthropologists and historians into collective apoplexy because they believe that people arrived in North America as far back as 16,000 B.C. So like I said before, I ALWAYS go with the Bible and you can make your own decision about what you think is right.

I also don't think it took thousands of years for the migration to finish taking place but more like a few centuries or so. One reason is that *The Scattering* from *Babel* was supernaturally inspired and secondly the Ice Age that was part of the environment would have pushed people southward fairly rapidly. Of course you need to keep in mind that I am neither anthropologist nor historian, but I have read the Bible a time or two and for me all of this has to fit the biblical time frame. Nobody knows how long it took for *The Scattering* to run its course but we know from the Bible that it started in the Middle East and the people scattered all over the earth eventually to the farthest tip of South America and to the farthest southern part of Africa and to any other place on the earth where God wanted for there to be people including those islands in the Caribbean Basin.

The Native Americans

By the time Columbus arrived in the New World in the year 1492, there were major groups of the "scattered" ones located throughout the area, and we now call them Native Americans. One of the most interesting aspects about almost all of those folks is that they were/are racially and ethnically related even though they were organized culturally into different tribes with different traditions and languages.

The original secular thinking was that the ancestry of all Native Americans was pretty much exclusively from East Asia. But of course we know from the Bible that it goes all the way back to *Babel* which wasn't in East Asia. It was in the Middle East! Eventually the Bible ALWAYS prevails after these differences show themselves and in this case the most recent DNA analyses on the subject have concluded that at least one-third of the ethnic heritage of almost all the groups of Native Americans goes back to West Eurasia which INCLUDES THE MIDDLE EAST. For people of faith it isn't necessary that the physical evidence always confirm the Bible. But when it eventually and inevitably does confirm it, it's worth reporting.

Christopher Columbus found Native Americans, direct descendants of *The Scattering*, living in the Caribbean Islands. Thinking that he had arrived on the outskirts of India and the Far East, he called the people "Indians" and that name has stuck through the centuries on an official level even though it has an inaccurate root. We'll learn more about that in the next article but for purposes of this one, you need to know that only twenty-seven years after Columbus' arrival in the New World, the first European explorer came to the Gulf Coast and he found a lot of Native Americans already living there. As the story goes he was most likely killed by one of those groups because he never made it back to his home base in Jamaica.

That first explorer was from Spain and before he disappeared into history, he managed to draw a map of the entire gulf coast which of course included the coast of the territory we now call Texas. When he arrived in 1519, a lot of folks descended from *The Scattering* were already living here.

The Native Texans

According to my research, the Texas territory is situated exactly at the joining place of two major cultural areas of Native Americans. Those areas are called by anthropologists the *Southwestern* and the *Plains* areas and the Texas part of that was occupied by three major cultures:

- The *Pueblo* from the upper Rio Grande region was centered to the western part of the area.
- The *Mound Builders* spread eastward from Texas to the Mississippi Valley and fathered the *Caddo Nation*.
- The *Mesoamericans* centered south of Texas and included Mexico and part of Central America.

No one culture was particularly dominant in Texas and over the centuries many different groups of people had inhabited the area for a time and moved on. After the arrival of the Europeans in the 16th century, the Native American tribes that lived at various times inside the boundaries of Texas include the Alabama, Apache, Atakapan, Bidai, Caddo, Coahuiltecan, Comanche, Cherokee, Choctaw, Coushatta, Hasinai, Jumano, Karankawa, Kickapoo, Kiowa, Tonkawa, and Wichita.

According to the experts, the bow and arrow appeared in Texas sometime during the 8th century A.D. and some of the "Indians" had begun to manufacture pottery. They also became increasingly dependent on bison for survival. Obsidian objects found in various sites in Texas confirm that some of the local tribes had trade relationships with cultures in present-day Mexico and the Rocky Mountains because that particular material isn't found locally. So it was either traded for or apprehended in some other way. By the time the Europeans started arriving though, the various cultures here had pretty much peaked in their technological development which put them at a disadvantage for defending themselves against the new folks that in the beginning were coming primarily from Spain.

Over the ensuing years much has been said about the idea that these Native Texans (and other Native Americans as well) were treated unfairly by the descendants of Europeans who migrated here. At the risk of being "politically incorrect," an important point to be made in this article is that the earth doesn't belong to people; it's God's (Psalm 24:1 and 1 Corinthians 10:26) and He can put whoever He wants to on His property with His ultimate purpose in mind: to expand His Kingdom on the earth.

For the most part the Indians of Texas were nomadic people who came and went as they pleased following after the great bison herds according to the seasons and the weather. With certain few exceptions, they didn't improve the lands they inhabited, but to be fair they also didn't do any damage. They followed no system of private ownership or stewardship other than some loosely-recognized tribal lands that were continuously shifting over the centuries. They developed no cities, no permanent civilizations, no agricultural interests, and no manufacturing ability beyond the stone-age levels they had been entrenched in for at least seven hundred years before the Europeans arrived. In sum, the Indians of Texas were developmentally stuck in a place that was below their God-given potential. As noble as the Native Texans might have been, they were not called or equipped to fulfill the purpose of God in the New World.

Nevertheless, to my way of thinking the Indians in Texas were/are a really important part of our history, a significant chapter in the Plan of God for this state. So I wanted to end this first article with a particular thought: when we think of Texas history we need to remember, to keep in mind that long before the Europeans came here the Indians were a part of the landscape. They had been here for thousands of years and had had children and grandchildren and tribes and cultures and battles and challenges and weather problems and unexpected deaths to contend with and questions about who they were and where they came from. Their blood is in the soil and history of Texas as much as any of the heroes we're more likely to celebrate. Don't' forget they were descended from people who were sent here by God as part of *The Scattering* and they had a divinely inspired purpose to contribute to our history. Said another way, the first Texans were Native Americans, aka American Indians; and they're as much a part of our history and the plan of God as anybody else that has ever come here.

If you think I'm being overly dramatic about it just consider that the name **Texas** was derived from a word in the Caddoan language of the Hasinai Culture. It means "friends" or "allies." It didn't come from the Spanish word *Tejas* as many people believe. No friend, both the Spanish and the English came from the Indian word *táysha'* which is a fitting legacy of those first Texans who came here so long ago and loved this place as much we do.

An artist's expression of Columbus'
1493 description of the Taino Indians

Aztec Indian from Mexico

Inca woman in Peru

Mayan Indian of Central America

Quechua woman in Ecuador

Inuit family dressed in caribou parkas

Apache

Caddo

Comanche

Cherokee

Hasinai

Jumano

Part Two:
The Europeans

Christianity as far as we know was first brought to Texas by explorers from Spain who had been sent out by their sovereign authority. They didn't come here accidently, they were sent out. And according to recorded history, the very first of those Europeans to set eyes on Texas was a certain *conquistador* by the name of *Alonso Alvarez de Pineda* who came for a visit in 1519 AD. Of course, at the time there were a lot of Native Americans here that had already discovered Texas and they liked it a lot. In fact, as we know from the previous article they had been roaming the far reaches of it for perhaps a couple of thousand years or so. Thus Texas had already experienced millennia of history before Don Alonso and the Europeans finally arrived for their first sighting.

A lot has been said about the exploitation and bloodshed and conquest the Europeans brought to the New World and emphasis is usually put on the fact that they had come looking for gold and worldly wealth. But history is never so simple and the fact is they brought something with them that actually changed the course of history. What they brought was their belief in a single Spirit God and His special Son who had died for all those Native Americans just as much as He had died for the Europeans. The effects of it didn't materialize overnight but in the context of history the arrival of Christianity in the New World brought about a relatively abrupt change. So we need to know right out of the box how it was that *Alonso Alvarez de Pineda* came to Texas and wound up being a part of something that changed everything.

The Ministry of Christopher Columbus

It turns out that *Don Alonso Alvarez de Pineda* came here leading an expedition by order of the governor of *Jamaica* of all places, for the purposes of finding a passageway between the Gulf of Mexico and Asia and to establish a first colony in whatever land area he was able to find. Apparently though he never got off the boat and of course he never quite found that secret passage to Asia either, but he did produce the first map of the northern Gulf Coast which is the earliest recorded document in Texas history. When you make a map of someplace you can bet others will soon follow looking for what's on the map, and that's exactly what happened in the years that followed Don Alonso's visit.

That Jamaican governor by the way was also a Spaniard and his name was *Francisco de Garay*. The only reason he was in Jamaica was because the Spanish had already come there with Christopher Columbus on his second voyage to the New World in 1494. They soon set up a colony and only twenty-five years later the governor sends out someone to look for Asia only to wind up "discovering" Texas.

16

So, history plainly shows a direct connection between that discovery and Christopher Columbus. It's important to see this connection because Columbus was a devout Christian who was accustomed to studying the Word and praying several times a day. Some modern secular historians these days are speculating on whether or not Columbus was actually a "Jew in hiding" but his personal writings over a long period of time clearly show that he was a devout and well-informed Christian. And according to all those studious and articulate writings of his, he believed *strongly* that God had singled him out and specifically called him to make all those voyages *for the purpose of spreading Christianity*. That's why many of the names he gave to the islands and other places he discovered were bible names that flowed out of his Christian world view. The first land he touched in 1492 in the Caribbean was an island in the Bahamas he named *San Salvador* which means literally "sainted Savior." So he wasn't in it so much for the gold and conquest although others around him might have been; no, according to his writings Christopher Columbus was intent on spreading Christianity around the entire world.

The whole thing about Christopher Columbus ever coming to the New World has the hand of God clearly on it even though secular historians want to write it off to coincidence and fate. Look, as best we know Columbus was an Italian from Genoa but for some reason historians aren't sure about that. He eventually went to Portugal for quite a while because he liked to sail ships down to Africa and at the time Portugal was the best place to do that from. With the experience he got there, he became convinced at some point that he could sail west and wind up in Japan and China instead of going east by the traditional, longer routes. But he needed funds to carry out that vision so in 1483 he went to see King John II of Portugal to ask for funds but was promptly rejected because it is thought that many influential people in Europe were having trouble accepting that the world was/is round even though the Bible had made note of that little geographic detail more than two thousand years before Columbus came on the scene (Isaiah 40:22). Columbus the Bible scholar had surely seen that scripture which would explain his confidence that was strong enough to fuel his dogged persistence for the following six years with repeated attempts to convince the reluctant King of Portugal to go along with his grand plan only to be rebuffed and publically ridiculed for his "strange" beliefs again and again.

At some point probably in 1489 (some think earlier), Columbus went to Spain to try to find a new source of funds. It took a while for Queen Isabella and King Ferdinand to override their doubts and most of their maritime advisors but something happened in early 1492 that brought it all together. In January of that year the Spanish took over Granada from the Moors finally ending 780 years of conflict between Christians and Muslims in the territory we now call Spain. The Christian victory in Granada freed up funds (including confiscated Muslim and Jewish properties) that Queen Isabella could consider using for this highly speculative idea Columbus had brought to her. When she thought he might go back to Portugal and give it another try over there, the deal was finally consummated and God's plan for the New World was put into action.

The point is this: here was an Italian who lived in Portugal now going to Spain, navigating through all those different languages to stubbornly insist on a trip that hardly anybody of that day believed was possible who needed a Christian victory in an eight hundred year old war to provide funds for a trip that would wind up changing the world. Indeed, the one trip he had to fight nine years for, the trip that almost NOBODY thought he would return from, turned out to be four trips from 1492 to 1504, and oh by the way: he also spoke and wrote in Latin which was a necessary component of all this history. All of this could not have been mere coincidence especially if you know how God works. Rather, it *had* to have all been part of a complex and organized master plan.

Among his writings Columbus wrote a famous book called *The Book of Prophecies* during the time between his third and fourth voyages to the New World that is an assemblage of Bible scriptures and related discussions he felt were particularly relevant to his God-given mission of discovery. What people believe is what then determines their interpretations of life and history, and it also inspires their vision and purpose in life. Columbus' own writings prove that he strongly believed that God had revealed in His Bible a plan that was to be applied to the entire world and that he was obeying the calling that God had specially ordained for his life when he set sail west across the Atlantic Ocean to spread Christianity to the rest of the world. His Christianity and biblical world view have been largely overlooked in the history that most of us have been exposed to and they explain a lot about what motivated him to do what he did.

Columbus was indeed a man of faith carrying out a mission to expand the Kingdom of God that called for him to venture into and across vast areas of uncharted oceans and places and then return back to the exact point he had started from which had never been done before. It took strong faith to confidently believe it could be done and it took the favor and direction of God to have actually done it successfully. Many people including most sea faring experts of the day expected him to fail, to be lost at sea and never return; but Christopher Columbus was no ordinary man because he believed he could do all things through Christ (Philippians 4:13).

But one thing to keep in mind is that Columbus wasn't a perfect man by any means. He made decisions for the benefit of Spain and in an effort to impress the King and Queen. He wanted them to receive a good return on their investment so there could be future voyages to the New World. And he decided to make slaves out of a few of the local "Indians" in the Caribbean and send them back to Spain although his writings reveal that his real objective was to lead them into Christianity after he had observed that they seemed to have no religion. No Christian is perfect but we understand that Christ makes us better than we would otherwise be. God is implementing His plan for the Kingdom of God to take over the earth, but He has to rely on imperfect people to get the job done. Even so, with all our imperfection and selfishness, the purposes of God somehow work out and His Kingdom advances. It was time for His Kingdom to come to the New World and Columbus turned out to be the one God used for that purpose.

In sum, the development of Texas can be traced back to a devout, studious Italian/Portuguese/Spanish/Latin-speaking Roman Catholic Christian with a vision to see the Kingdom of God covering the whole earth and a willingness to submit to the plan of God for his life even though others, the experts and sovereigns of the day made fun of him and even though the implementation of his plan would put his life at risk. He was confident that God had called him and by strong faith he pursued his calling. He discovered Jamaica in 1494 while in the act of spreading Christianity and 25 years later a man was sent from there to map the Gulf coast as he looked for a passage to Asia. With the making of that map a door was opened and the stage was set for God Almighty to send His people into the rest of the world to spread the Gospel to the people He had begun "scattering" there thousands of years earlier.

Columbus made two additional trips to the New World: from 1498 to 1500 and from 1502 to 1504, a total of four trips. He pretty much stayed among the Caribbean islands and visited/discovered/explored in particular Hispaniola (Dominican Republic and Haiti), Puerto Rico, Cuba, the Bahamas, Jamaica and along the coasts of Mexico, Central America and northern South America. In that process he lived a great adventure, fulfilled the calling of God on his life and changed the ENTIRE world forever.

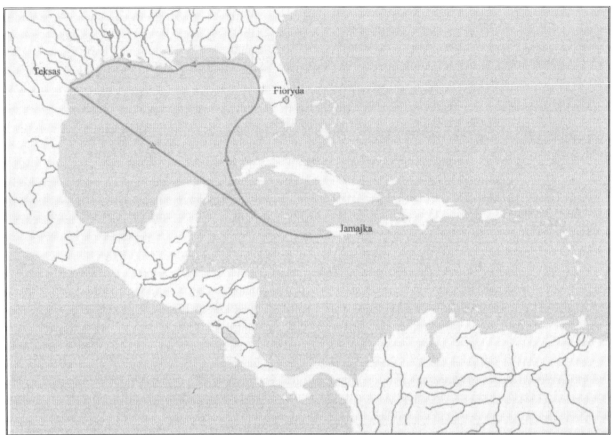

The Voyage of Alonso Alvarez de Pineda in 1519

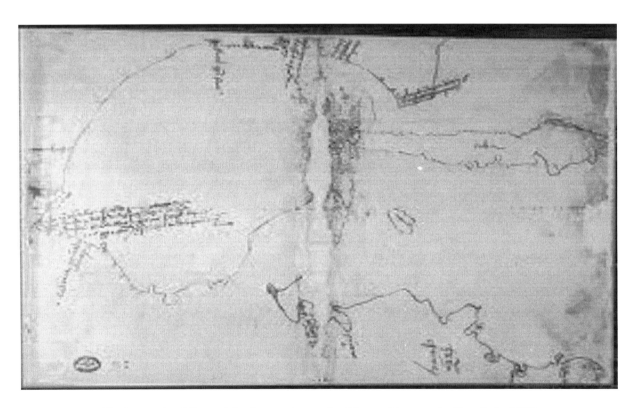

Photograph of the original map drawn by Alonso Alvarez de Pineda in 1519

20

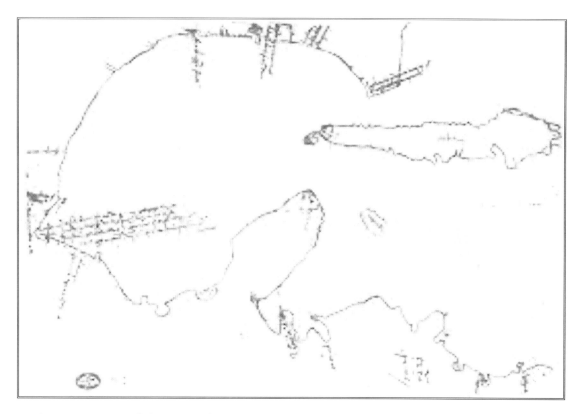

Easier to see copy of the original map drawn by De Pineda in 1519 of the Gulf coast showing the coast line of Texas on the left, around to Florida on the right which can be seen just over the island of Cuba with the Mexican Yucatan Peninsula to the south

Copy of a painting of the famous Alonso Alvarez de Pineda who drew the first map of the Texas coast line in 1519 without ever getting off his boat.
He also never made it back to Jamaica.

Christopher Columbus's Four Voyages

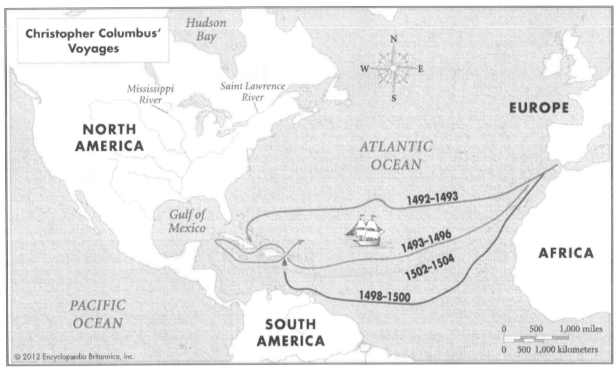

Columbus, Christopher: Columbus's voyages. Map/Still. *Britannica Online for Kids*. Web. 25 Apr. 2014.
<http://kids.britannica.com/elementary/art-88703>.

© 2014 Encyclopædia Britannica, Inc.

A popular painted likeness of Christopher Columbus by
Sebastian del Piombo in 1520. There is no known painting from life of Columbus.

A likeness of the Santa Maria, the principal vessel of
Christopher Columbus on his first voyage to the New World

Part Three:
The Conquistadores

So far in our story we've seen the first European come to Texas, *Alonso Alvarez de Pineda* in the year 1519. He came originally from Spain and eventually to Texas leading an expedition of four ships and 270 men under orders from the governor of Jamaica to find a passage to Asia and to establish a colony in the area that was to become Texas.

We've also seen how this "discovery" fit into an overall plan that God had implemented to expand His Kingdom on the earth as we connected the "discovery" of Texas back to the second voyage of Christopher Columbus in 1494. As we now know Columbus was a dedicated and committed Christian who believed he was called by God to spread Christianity to the rest of the world. And as it turned out, Texas was squarely in the path of that plan.

Now *Alonso Alvarez de Pineda* was the first of a very special group of men who came to be known as *Los Conquistadores* or in English "The Conquerors." In those early years several of them crisscrossed the area we now call Texas exploring, discovering, developing, impacting, and yes also conquering whatever and whoever they ran into. Their effects on our history were profound and helped mold for us the unique character of history we like to talk and brag about so much.

Alonso Alvarez de Pineda never found that passage to Asia he was looking for and he didn't establish the colony he'd been told to get started. But he did wind up drawing a map of the northern Gulf Coast even though he apparently never got off his boat the whole time he was here. It seems he soon crossed paths with a rival *conquistador* by the name of *Hernan Cortes* who didn't want Don Alonso in the area and chased him out. By all accounts *Cortes* was one tough *hombre* which is probably why Don Alonso never got off his boat. He *did* accomplish one important thing though before he was killed mysteriously probably by Indians: he put Texas on the map.

The Influence of Hernan Cortes

Now we need to talk a little more about this second *Conquistador, Hernan Cortes* because he had perhaps the greatest impact on Texas history of any of them even though like Don Alonso he never set foot here. Rather, he wound up operating down south in what is now called Mexico and in the summer of 1520 he conquered the entire Aztec nation, killed their king *Montezuma II* and destroyed *Tenochtitlan* their capital city that had been constructed on the site of what is present day Mexico City. The Aztecs had been in charge down there for more than 200 years but suddenly they lost their power and *Hernan Cortes* became the man in charge.

There was a lot of death and brutality involved in what *Cortes* did down there. But there was also a Christian influence on that event that historians often overlook. The facts are that *Cortes* and his expedition, even as they were initially trying to befriend and coexist with the Aztecs, had witnessed their routine practice of sacrificing women and children and their Catholic values wouldn't let them tolerate it. So, they decided to put a stop to it and were able to acquire the manpower support of some sympathetic local native tribes in the area that had been taken over by the Aztecs and didn't like human sacrifice either. Secular historians tend to overlook this important factoid and miss this connection of Christianity to those early days of Texas history.

So, what is now the country of Mexico suddenly came under the rule of Spain. And after that, it was Cortes who was responsible for building Mexico City on top of the ruins of *Tenochtitlan*, for introducing the Spanish language into the local culture and for starting the Roman Catholic evangelization of not only the native populations in Mexico but eventually also down into Central America apparently as far as present-day Honduras and Nicaragua. That evangelization program was to be greatly expanded later with the coming of the Franciscans but more on that in the next article.

To sum up, Cortes apparently never got to Texas physically but Texas history was significantly impacted by what he did down in Mexico. He was responsible for initiating some important changes: he changed the culture, he changed the language and he changed the religion; and all of that wound up changing the history of Texas over the following three centuries and beyond. And oh by the way: he was never authorized by the King of Spain to do all the conquering and building that he undertook; he just did it and got the authorization later. Cortes got a lot of results accomplished but it was probably a good idea to stay away from his area while he was working on them.

The Ones Who Actually Got Here

Spain was soon on the move all over the area and a series of *conquistadores* began to arrive in Texas and exert their influence. The first Europeans known to have actually set foot on Texas soil were the survivors of an ill-fated expedition led by *Pánfilo de Narváez* and consisting of 400 Spanish soldiers and 82 horses that had been dispatched from Cuba to explore Florida. After surviving one Caribbean hurricane they got caught in a later storm in 1528 and only 80 survivors NOT including the unfortunate *Narvaez* who was drowned at sea were finally washed ashore in Galveston Bay. He didn't quite get here but those 80 survivors were the first Europeans to actually arrive in Texas.

By 1534 only four out of those 80 survivors were still alive due to the ravages of sickness and hardship. Two of the four included *Álvar Núñez Cabeza de Vaca*, who had been the second in command of the original expedition under *Narvaez*, and an African slave named *Estevanico*. Fearing they would soon die too if they stayed in the Galveston area, the four remaining survivors struck out across Texas following the Gulf Coast westward eventually crossing the lower Rio Grande River into Mexico and continuing overland to Mexico City. That part of the trip took about 18 months, a total of 8 years and 6.000 miles if you go back to the start of the expedition in Florida, and they became the first Europeans to explore the interior of Texas.

While they were traveling along they kept hearing from the various local native groups they encountered about a legend involving seven cities of gold known as *Cibola*. Of course *Cabeza de Vaca* made it a point to repeat the legend to the Spanish officials they ran into on the border and in Mexico City and back in Spain when he returned there to regroup. The result was that a whole bunch of other folks soon came around looking for those seven golden cities.

The next big name to come to Texas was none other than the great explorer *Francisco Vásquez de Coronado* and he came chasing after those *Seven Cities*. In January 1540, *Antonio de Mendoza* the viceroy of New Spain in Mexico City commissioned Coronado to go look for the gold and sent him along with an expedition that included 1,000 foot soldiers, 300 horsemen, several priests, 1,500 horses and mules plus some accompanying rather large herds of cattle and sheep. When he got to those seven cities over in the Arizona–New Mexico area, he couldn't find any gold but he soon heard about another stash off toward the northeast that he could chase after in a place called *Quivira* so he set out after that in April of 1541. Eventually they crossed the Pecos River and continued on to the West Texas Plains where they were amazed at the number of buffalo they saw. None of the other Europeans had mentioned buffalo before. Eventually *Coronado* and his group reached Palo Duro Canyon near present day Amarillo and went on up into Kansas looking for *Quivira* but there wasn't any gold there either. So after he killed the man who had told him about *Quivira*, the great *Coronado* had to admit defeat and report back to the Viceroy that no gold could be found.

After it was reported that even Coronado with that huge expedition of his couldn't find any gold, interest in new expeditions pretty much dried up. And there had been a few other explorers that had also been unsuccessful looking for gold in places outside of Texas as well. But there was one last *conquistador* just after Coronado who came west from Florida, Georgia, Alabama, Mississippi and Arkansas and then ventured into Texas in 1542. His name was *Luis de Moscoso de Alvaredo* and he had originally been under the command of *Hernando de Soto* but De Soto died in the midst of all that exploring and never made it to Texas. So Don Luis took over and headed west in an attempt to find an overland route back to Mexico City. Eventually he crossed over into Texas at about where Texarkana is today. But things got too tough for him so he turned around and went back to the Mississippi River where he and his men built some boats and sailed back to Mexico City by going down the river and into the Gulf. He didn't find any gold either and lost half his men, but he *did* do a lot of exploring.

And that was pretty much the end of the Spanish *Conquistador* activity in Texas even though a few of them were still exploring in other places outside of Texas like New Mexico and Arizona.

Of course, wherever they went they brought their Christianity and their language with them and wound up profoundly impacting the history and the culture of Texas in ways that are obviously still with us today. Eventually when they couldn't find any gold after investing a lot of money looking for it, the Spanish political and financial powers lost interest in this area for a while which set the stage for the coming of the Franciscans.

Hernan Cortes looking really spiffy here changed Mexican and Texas history by introducing the Spanish language and Christianity in the New World

Route of infamous Conquistador Hernan Cortes in his conquest and rebuilding of Mexico

The route of Pánfilo de Narváez up until he left on a raft attempting to return to Cuba and disappeared never to be seen again

The unfortunate Pánfilo de Narváez... drowned at sea after antagonizing most of the Native Americans on Florida's west coast

A rather stern looking conquistador by the name of Álvar Núñez Cabeza de Vaca survived two major storms to be among the first Europeans to set foot in Texas on his way from the southeast end of Cuba all the way to Mexico City

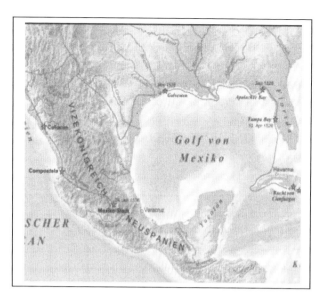

The route of the persistent, never-give-up, determined explorer Cabeza de Vaca

Estevanico was an African slave, one of four people to survive the expedition of Panfilo de Narvaez. After an 8 year ordeal he was sold to Mex. Viceroy Antonio de Mendoza and sent out again to look for Cibola, killed at age 39 by Zuni Indians.

Adventures in the Unknown Interior of America (1542)

This is the cover of Cabeza de Vaca's report to the King of Spain about his trip to the Americas that took the lives of everyone except himself and three other men out of a total of 300 and cost him 8 years of his life and 6,000 miles of hardship.

Portrait of Coronado one of the truly great
Conquistadores who came across the panhandle of Texas looking for the Seven
Cities of Cibola the mythical golden
cities NEVER found by anybody...
an Indian joke maybe?

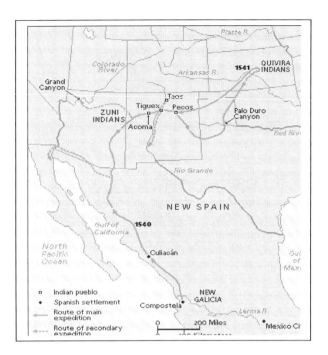

Coronado came all the way up from Mexico
to Arizona with side trips to lower California
on the west and New Mexico on the east
and then across Texas and on to Kansas
seeking Quivira which wasn't found
either, a total trip of 4,000 miles

Coronado was the first European to see the wonders of the Grand Canyon
and the first to shoot buffalo while he searched for the Seven Cities of Cibola

He looked everywhere for those seven cities of gold but unsuccessfully. When Coronado finally gave up after not finding Quivira or anything else of value, he returned to Spain with serious money troubles and some scratches on his illustrious reputation. But he paved the way for a lot of Franciscans who stayed in Texas or came later.

When Coronado got to where he thought the seven cities were, he had to fight the Indians there only to find out that there was no gold anywhere after he finally won the battle.

Luis de Moscoso de Alvaredo...
He took up the journey after De Soto died
And made it all the way to Texas

Hernando de Soto...
One of the greatest of the explorers but died
before he could make it to Texas

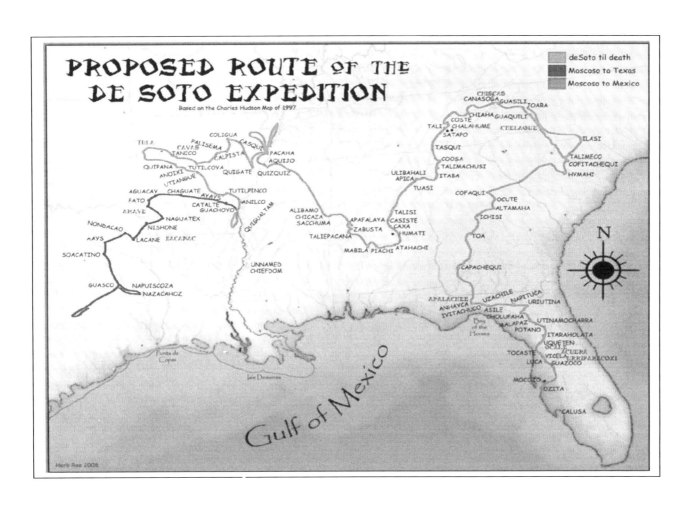

Part Four:
The Franciscans

As we begin Part Four keep in mind that the purpose of this series is to highlight the influence of Christianity on the unique history and culture of Texas. It's not one of those deep scholarly treatises, but what we're trying to do is focus on the observation that the development of Texas was part of a great plan of God to develop and settle the New World tracing back to Christopher Columbus and even before him.

The first Europeans who came here were Roman Catholics and as a group they were a relatively religious people. According to the Bible a Christian by definition is someone who has confessed Jesus Christ as Lord, who believes in his/her heart in His resurrection (Romans 10:9) and has become a disciple i.e., a *follower* of the Faith (Matthew 28:19). Indeed then, most of the early European arrivals in Texas would have professed these qualifications and called themselves Christians. Did some of them do some unchristian things while they were visiting the Texas territory? Yes they did, but thank goodness sin does not disqualify us from our Christianity or we would ALL be in a heap of trouble. Being a Christian is not about what we DO so much and it's not about theology; it's about what He does/has done and the spiritual condition of our inner person. In sum then, the early arrivals professed to be Roman Catholic Christians and they professed it fervently.

One of the characteristics of Christianity is that we always seek to make available to non-believers the special relationship we have with God through Jesus Christ. Thus evangelism is a key part of our faith and over the centuries it has taken on various forms: some were scriptural and some not so scriptural. The point is though that Christians will always seek to make converts which happened to some extent under the influence of the *Conquistadores* even though their higher priorities had been to find gold, to claim territories for the rule of Spain and to eradicate resistance whenever it arose.

When they didn't find the gold after a number of optimistic attempts, the Spanish lost interest for a while in the "northern frontier" including the Texas territory. There were no colonies to worry about, no forts to defend and no particular plans for expansion or immigration. Nothing of permanence had been established. But finally after about 40 years of malaise, their attitude started to change between 1578 and 1580 about the time the English explorer Sir Francis Drake set sail for the Americas. That development got their attention because the Spanish saw him as a competitor. Consequently they made the decision finally to establish Spanish colonies up north somewhere but still it took a number of years to get things moving because the pot of gold that had motivated folks in previous years was no longer considered to be a practical attraction to investors for financing the necessary expeditions. This time though it wasn't *Conquistadores* who would try to lead the colonization. Rather it was the Spanish Roman Catholic clergy represented for the most part by members of the *Franciscan* order who worked faithfully for more than 200 years to establish and operate a system of as many as 27 missions, depending on how you count them, at various times and places around the Texas territory.

The Spanish colonization program was really slow to get going but finally in early 1598, *Juan de Oñate* set out with 400 men plus some of their families, a herd of 7,000 horses, cattle, and sheep and a group of Catholic priests. Their objective was to establish a colony somewhere in the northern frontier but they must have had a hard time finding the right place because they didn't get it started until 1610. That first one though became Santa Fe, New Mexico and from that key colony the Franciscans were able to send out groups both west and east. The ones that went east crossed into the Texas Panhandle but none of them established a colony or anything "permanent" in Texas until about 1630.

Now before going any further with them into Texas history, we need to be clear about the priorities of the Franciscan colonization effort. They didn't go and do all this work for the purpose of finding gold although if they had accidently found some they wouldn't have turned it down. But their first priority was to evangelize the local populations of Native Americans. That was no easy task because most of the native populations were nomadic and there were a lot of different affiliations to try to work with. All these different groups had varying aspects among their particular cultures, including language variations and even ancient rivalries that the Franciscans had to learn about, sift through and deal with in order to get to their objectives.

It also wasn't an easy task because most Native Americans were ALREADY a religious people and at first they didn't want to change religions just because some Europeans came around and told them they ought to. And so, there's a fundamental point to be made here: many folks tend to look down on those original 17th century Texas folks as backward, combative non-believers that many called *savages*. But that's not the best focus. Rather, the better way of looking at this moment in history comes from asking this question: what was the one main thing that actually COMPELLED all those Franciscans to come into Texas and change our history *and* our culture here for all time? It was the fact that there were thousands of people in the established local populations who needed to be evangelized, who needed to know Jesus. If that need had not been there then Spanish expansion within the New World could have been delayed for centuries or passed over to other countries like France and England. Franciscans carried the load for Spanish colonization and they were driven by the spiritual need of the native population. They were uniquely qualified to bring Jesus to the New World because they were after all clergy, trained in the Bible for the precise purpose they wound up pursuing. Is it too hard to believe that God just might have wanted as many of those local Native American non-believers as possible to come to know Jesus?

The first missionary attempts into Texas occurred in 1629 and again in 1632 by *Father Juan de Salas* leading a small group of missionaries and soldiers from the mission in Santa Fe to work among the Jumano tribal group in the area near present-day San Angelo. To be sure these were brief excursions and were said to have been requested by the *Jumano* "Indians" in West Texas for the purpose of religious instruction which doesn't seem quite plausible somehow but that's what history says. Interestingly though, the *Jumanos* were already demonstrating a basic knowledge of Christianity when the Franciscans arrived there that they attributed to the teachings of the "Woman in Blue." History says she was a Spanish Franciscan nun by the name of *María de Jesús de Agreda* who appeared to the Native Americans in their "present-day" Texas and New Mexico through "bilocation." She never left Spain and yet the *Jumanos* knew her BEFORE the Franciscans arrived in San Angelo. Hey! God moves however He wants to so don't be putting this down too quickly unless you're sure about it. Despite Sister Maria's "bilocation" ministry though, neither of these earliest excursions produced anything permanent like a colony or a mission.

Actually it took another 50 years before the Franciscans could finally make something "permanent" happen in the Texas territory. In 1682 the first two Spanish missions were established and we've included a list of 25 of the Texas missions and their dates of establishment at the end of this chapter. In total there were approximately 27 or so missions established within the current boundaries of the State of Texas, by far the most in the northern territory. It's hard to get a really accurate count though because some of them failed after a few years and others were relocated and duplicated. So the list at the end of this chapter is approximately accurate without going into a more in-depth study which is beyond the scope of this series of articles. Approximately 4 of the missions were established near the end of the 17th century and the remainder in the 18th century.

Now mixed up in all of this story about the Franciscans is that one of the six flags over Texas, as most Texans know, was the French flag; and as it turned out, when the French became interested in eastern Texas after they had started their own colonization in what is now Louisiana, it caused the Franciscans to start establishing missions on a priority basis in the east to head off this new competitor. And here's the way that happened.

In 1684, a French nobleman *René-Robert Cavelier, Sieur de La Salle,* founded a colony on the Texas Gulf Coast called *Fort Saint Louis*. Why were the French interested in expanding westward? Certainly it was to increase their sovereign territory in the New World, but also according to their journals it was to evangelize the Native Americans in East Texas. As it turned out the French colonies weren't successful and after La Salle's murder they were soon abandoned. An interesting part of history is that during the time of these missions, there was no official French flag so that's why you can see a number of different designs for the French flag used in displays of the "six flags over Texas."

The French presence didn't last very long but it was long enough to get into the 6-flag group and it was long enough to shock the Spanish into action. Keep in mind this was back in the 17th century so the Spanish weren't even aware of LaSalle's expansion projects until 1689 when they finally discovered the remains of *Fort Saint Louis* near Matagorda Bay. La Salle was already dead and the fort abandoned when it was discovered but the knowledge that the French had been there for five years without anybody knowing about it got people's attention. That's when the Franciscans suddenly started two missions in 1689-90 and everything the Franciscans worked on in East Texas after that was in direct response to their fear of another French encroachment.

Before leaving this subject, let's get a brief idea of what life was like in the Franciscan missions. What were their objectives and how did those tie in to our subject of examining the influence of Christianity on Texas history?

Mission Life

Now if you want to know more about the development and construction of all these Spanish missions, you can find a lot of information on the Internet and among a host of other historical resources as well. All of that detail is very interesting but it's not a part of this series. Nevertheless, if it's information you want, there really is a lot available for history buffs to study and then go by all means to visit some of the remains of these missions to see the history first hand. It's a fascinating attraction and worth the time to travel around our state and experience history while imagining yourself involved in the particular mission you are visiting. Had you been living there in the 17th and 18th centuries, here's a glimpse at how your life would have been.

Overall what the Franciscan missionaries tried to do was make life within the mission communities resemble Spanish villages and culture which was obviously a far-cry from what Native Americans had been used to. In their new environment they were expected to mature in Roman Catholic Christianity, the Spanish language and the understanding of Spanish political and economic matters. Also, an essential part of their conversion was to learn vocational skills such as farming, blacksmithing, weaving, masonry and carpentry so they could become Spanish citizens and productive inhabitants of their missions.

The underlying idea was that after a time the various mission communities would mature sufficiently to become ordinary Spanish colonial societies involving an official transition called "secularization." In that process the mission's communal properties were privatized and the direction of civil life became a secular affair in the sense that the direction of church life was transferred from the missionary religious orders like the Franciscans to the Catholic diocesan church. Although colonial law didn't specify a precise time for this transition to be carried out, increasing pressure for the secularization of most missions developed in the last decades of the 18th century.

An Overall Evaluation

An overall evaluation of the Spanish Missions in the history of Texas would probably be that the mission system wasn't able to deliver the results that had been hoped for. In fact, most of them shut down a few years after they started and others were moved to secondary locations as the Franciscans struggled to convert the Texas territory into their version of New Spain. What they _did_ do though was bring Christianity to thousands of Native Americans over a span of perhaps 150 years or so which set the stage for what was to come later. The missions also significantly reduced in their areas of influence the abuse and exploitation of Native Americans that characterized other places that were under secular control. And in the final analysis the history and culture of Texas were forever connected to our unique Franciscan Christian influence and these special missions. Remember folks: one of those missions is the ALAMO!

LIST OF FRANCISCAN MISSIONS IN TEXAS

Name	Date Established
• Mission Nuestra Señora de la Limpia Concepción de Los Piros de Socorro del Sur	1682
• Mission Corpus Christi de la Ysleta del Sur	1682
• Mission San Francisco de la Espada	1689
• Mission Santísimo Nombre de María	1690
• Mission Nuestra Señora de la Purísima Concepción de Acuña	1716
• Mission San José de los Nazonis (Later moved to San Antonio)	1716
• Mission Nuestra Señora de Guadalupe de los Nacogdoches	1716
• Mission Nuestra Señora de los Dolores de los Ais	1717
• Mission San Miguel de Linares de los Adaes	1717
• Mission San Antonio de Valero **(The Alamo)**	1718
• Mission San José y San Miguel de Aguayo	1720
• Mission Nuestra Señora del Espíritu Santo de Zúñiga	1722
• Mission San Francisco Xavier de Nájera	1722
• Mission Santa Maria de las Caldas	1730
• Mission San Juan Capistrano (Relocated from East Texas)	1731
• Mission San Francisco Xavier de Horcasitas	1745
• Mission San Ildefonso	1746
• Mission Nuestra Senora de la Candelaria del Canon	1749
• Mission Nuestra Señora del Rosario	1754
• Mission Nuestra Señora de Guadalupe	1756
• Mission San Francisco Xavier de los Dolores	1756
• Mission Nuestra Señora de la Luz	1756
• Mission Santa Cruz de San Sabá	1757
• Mission San Lorenzo de la Santa Cruz	1762
• Mission Nuestra Señora del Refugio	1793

THE GREAT MISSIONS OF TEXAS:

The best known of them all: THE ALAMO located in San Antonio, Texas
Also known as: Mission San Antonio de Valero

Mission San Jose in San Antonio

Mission Concepcion in San Antonio

**Mission San Francisco de la Espada
in San Antonio**

Mission San Juan in San Antonio

Mission Ysleta in El Paso

Mission Espirito Santo in Goliad

Inside Mission San Francisco de Espada

MISSION LIFE IN EARLY TEXAS AS EXPRESSED BY OUR ARTISTS:

"Ascension Thursday" by Stefan Kramar depicts
Fray Juan de Padilla, who accompanied the Coronado Expedition

"The Missionaries as They Came and Went"

Ministering to the Native Americans

Native Americans implementing their new farming skills

Part Five:
The Settlers

So far in this series we've mostly talked about the Spanish and the Native Americans who had taken up residence in Texas. A few French folks also came along for a short time but by 1690 their main effort in East Texas had fizzled and they went back home to Louisiana. The Spanish made sure that would be the end of it by establishing some of their missions to intersect with the French entryway which pretty much left that part of the northern territory occupied by just a few Spanish settlers, a few Franciscans and a lot of Native Americans. The one noteworthy exception a few years later was the notorious French pirate _Jean Laffite_ and his small group of high seas desperados who occupied Galveston Island from 1817 to 1820 and used it as the headquarters for their pirating and smuggling operations. But they weren't really settlers,

There _was_ a third group of folks who _were_ settlers though. They were comprised of a few locals who were the descendants of Spanish soldiers and families that had originally come to New Spain, stayed in the area around what is now central _Mexico_ and mixed with the Indian populations to produce succeeding generations of folks who slowly gravitated up north. As you might expect they were called _Mexicans_ in those days and a few of them came up into the northern frontier and settled here during the time of the Franciscans but not under their direct control. Some of them worked as hands and servants in the missions or for other endeavors of the Spanish but according to historians they were seen as lacking essential skills and were looked down upon as inferior along with the Native Americans.

By the year 1790 around the time those last missions were being built, the entire settler population of this vast Texas territory was estimated to be only about 2,500 people. Part of the reason for the sparseness was the relative hostility of some of the local Native American tribes in comparison to other places like New Mexico and California where pacification had been more successful and settlers had consequently been drawn to those areas in much greater numbers. Some of the Native American groups here didn't want more settlers in Texas, but the Spanish DID want them and they especially wanted settlers from America so they could help stabilize the northern borders. And so, in the late 18th and early 19th centuries American settlers began gradually filtering into the territory and initially they weren't opposed by the Spanish authorities who weren't that available around the area anyway.

Soon after that between 1820 and 1835 the real Anglo-American colonization of Texas finally got going and the settler population grew to over 38,000. Relatively speaking, that was a big number and the settlers were particularly attracted to inexpensive land that was first made available by Spanish land grant in 1820. Undeveloped land in the United States land offices cost $1.25 an acre for a minimum of 80 acres ($100) payable at the time of purchase. But in Texas each head of a family, male or female, could claim a _"head right"_ of 4,605 acres (4,428 acres of grazing land plus177 acres of irrigable farm land) at a cost of about four cents per acre ($184) payable in six years, and even that low sum was reduced later on by the authorities. Just a year later in 1821, Mexico won its independence from Spain but this same Spanish immigration program was continued by the new government and the flow of settlers into the territory dramatically increased. <u>Most of them were Protestants</u>.

How Protestants Came to the New World

Now before we go any farther, this is another good place to look more closely for God's hand on that larger, intelligently designed plan for the New World we discussed in previous articles. Do you remember that first European back in *Part Two* by the name of *Alonso Alvarez de Pineda* who came to see Texas back in 1519? Well just two years before that in 1517, *Martin Luther* had posted his 95 theses at *All Saints' Castle Church* in Wittenberg, Germany objecting to the selling of indulgences and that little event precipitated nothing less than the *Protestant Reformation*.

Consider this confluence of events for a moment: at virtually the same time the Protestant Reformation is beginning in Europe (1517) that first European is "discovering" a place in 1519 where only three hundred years later Protestant settlers would be clamoring to settle. Where did all those settlers come from to respond to the Spanish and Mexican land grant programs? Well, only about 100 years after the Reformation, the first <u>Protestant</u> colonies had been established on the eastern seaboard of North America. The first ones were St. Augustine, Roanoke, Jamestown, Plymouth, and Massachusetts Bay. And it's important to know that they came to the New World in search of religious freedom and a place where they could develop their new-found Protestantism.

Keep in mind that before 1517 the only Christianity in Western Europe except for a few small clandestine remnant groups here and there was essentially Roman Catholicism. For Eastern Europe and a few places in Asia, Orthodox Christianity that had split off from Roman Catholicism was available from Constantinople. And that was pretty much the Christian world at the time Martin Luther decided to "propose" a few changes. Leading up to that were some really important developments that helped make possible the Protestant explosion that was about to be released and served to confirm that God Almighty had a Master Plan that was working out just fine. And, there were some other key things that happened *during* the birth of this new movement that also helped it along. Without these key things happening, the result of Luther's "proposal" might have been slower, later and less explosive that what actually happened:

- In 1382 against the wishes of the Catholic Church, John Wycliffe became the first person to translate the entire Bible into English. This monumental event made the Bible available for the first time in the native language of the very people whose descendants would become the Protestants that ultimately colonized the New World. Even so, the Wycliffe translation had to be hand-copied so its rate of dissemination was somewhat restricted. But it was a beginning for getting the Bible into the hands of regular people.

- In 1454 Johannes Gutenberg printed an edition of the Latin Vulgate Bible on the first moveable-type printing press in Mainz, Germany. With this new way of printing, books could be copied faster and cheaper than ever before, a fact that Protestants soon took advantage of. Within a hundred years there was a virtual explosion of Protestant Bibles coming off the new presses. Keep in mind that less than 40 years later, Columbus would set sail for the New World believing he had been called by God to spread the Gospel to the nations of the world.

- In 1525 as the Reformation was taking hold, William Tyndale completed an English translation of the New Testament from the Greek, which church authorities in England tried their best to confiscate and burn. Eventually he was arrested, spent over a year in jail and was then strangled and burned at the stake near Brussels on October 6, 1536. It's estimated that some 90 percent of the New Testament in the 1611 King James Bible that was the foundation of the colonization of the New World was the work of this brave and determined martyr.

- Even though Tyndale was unable to complete his translation of the Old Testament before his death, one of his assistants Miles Coverdale completed it using Martin Luther's German text and the Latin translation as sources, and in Germany he printed the first complete Bible in English on October 4, 1535.

- In 1534 the Church of England officially separated from the Roman Catholic Church but became an additional persecutor of the Protestant movement.

The power of the Protestant Reformation came from regular Believers finally having access to the Word of God. And the Catholic Church stood firmly against that access. So, it wasn't long before the first Protestant groups started trying to come to the New World seeking religious freedom and in 1565, a group of French Huguenots (Protestants) established a small colony near the future location of St. Augustine, Florida. Unfortunately, the Spanish king responded to this "trespass" by sending 1000 troops and 11 ships to destroy the infant colony. The Huguenots were summarily overwhelmed and all but a few were killed on September 25, 1565.

That set the stage for the great move of Protestants that would soon come from England and wind up doing something special in the New World. Their descendants would forge a new nation on the wave of the first *Great Awakening* (1731–1755) and provide the impetus for a population of Protestant settlers yearning to move west to seek a new destiny during the second *Great Awakening* (1790–1840). There were four initial colonies that got this all started:

- The first was known as the *Roanoke Colony* and was established on Roanoke Island off the coast of present-day North Carolina on July 4, 1584. It had been organized and funded by Sir Walter Raleigh and Queen Elizabeth I and the principal leader of the expedition was Phillip Amadas. Although there were several attempts to make this colony prosper, it eventually failed for unknown reasons, in fact the colonists mysteriously disappeared on two different occasions, and it is known today as the *Lost Colony of Roanoke*.

- The next attempt was the *Jamestown Colony* established on May 4, 1607 on the east coast of present day Virginia. Even though Captain John Smith became the more famous, the first president of the colony was actually Captain Edward Maria-Wingfield and he is known today as the *Father of Virginia*. Smith was actually the third president and had to return to England in 1609 because he had been severely burned in an explosion. The Jamestown colonists were largely entrepreneurs unaccustomed to agriculture and hard labor and they had a difficult time getting started. But they did indeed prevail and became the first permanent English colony in the New World.

- The second permanent colony was the *Plymouth Colony* that was begun December 16, 1620 by English Separatists who arrived on the *Mayflower* and came to be known as *Pilgrims*. They were a part of an English *Congregationalist* group led by William Bradford that had fled from Scrooby, England to the Netherlands in 1609 because of religious persecution. Although half of their number died during the first winter In Massachusetts, they prevailed with the help of local Native Americans and eventually became a successful colony. It was eventually absorbed into the *Massachusetts Bay Colony* in 1691.

- The most successful of these four initial colonies was the *Massachusetts Bay Colony* that was started in 1628 near the present-day cities of Salem and Boston. The population which grew to 20,000 during the 1630's was mostly *Puritan* and its governance was dominated by a small group of leaders who were strongly influenced by *Puritan* religious leaders. As a consequence, the colonial leadership exhibited intolerance toward other religious views including Anglicans, Quakers, and Baptists. But the business of the colony was expertly led by John Winthrop after his arrival in 1630.

And so, by the time the *First Great Awakening* came along in 1731 the English colonial development in the New World was well in progress. The *Great Awakenings* were SIGNIFICANT moves of God where millions of people came to know Jesus in a personal way. According to historians they *deeply* influenced the future development of the United States in a relatively short period of time by changing the way Christian believers looked at their relationship with God, by developing the strength and character of the individual and by giving the new confederation of colonies a sense of united purpose and destiny.

They also helped to establish individual religious experience over traditional intellectual-based church doctrine and to decrease the relative importance and weight of the clergy and the local church. New denominations arose or grew in numbers as a result of the emphasis on individual faith and salvation, and the believers who came out of the Great Awakenings were much stronger both spiritually and individually than the ones who went into them. Those Great Awakenings helped instill a world view in the hearts and minds of succeeding generations of Protestants who would be called upon to take their brand of Christianity across the continent.

The First Great Awakening prepared the colonists for the creation of a new nation less than 20 years later by drawing the colonies together under a common purpose and plan, by establishing a new spiritual base on which to build that new nation and by emphasizing that God works through individuals to build His Kingdom. The *Declaration of Independence* that was written in 1776 and introduced the new nation to the world reflects many biblical principles for Christian life that came out of *The First Great Awakening*. And through that it provided the underpinnings for a group of tough, persistent, risk-taking, Protestant Christians who had been adequately prepared to go out and settle in new worlds that they themselves had found and developed and established with the help of God.

John Wycliffe

Johannes Gutenberg

William Tyndale

Martin Luther

Edward Maria-Wingfield
Jamestown Colony (1607)

William Bradford
Plymouth Colony (1620)

John Winthrop
Massachusetts Bay (1630)

The Rise of Protestantism in Texas

As the *Second Great Awakening* (1790-1840) developed and it became evident that American settlers would gravitate to the western territories, evangelical churches and preachers were in the forefront of that movement. Their goal was to see that the Gospel of the Kingdom was carried by the Anglo-American advance across the continent. Geographically the Texas territory was directly in the path of this great move of God. As we go forward into this great story, keep the following backdrop summary in mind:

- Spanish and Mexican law established a one-church system: Catholics only.

- The Spanish and Mexican governments *did* want Anglo-American settlers to settle in Texas to stabilize the environment and future growth of the territory.

- Most of the Anglo settlers who came into Texas to take advantage of low land prices and a chance to start over were Protestants.

As it turned out the move of God was way stronger than the manmade law. Protestantism made its first inroads into Texas between 1815 and 1817 and here are some important highlights. In extreme Northeast Texas, which was considered to be part of Arkansas at that time, circuit-riding <u>Methodist</u> preachers made trips into the region. In 1815, Methodist William Stevenson began preaching in private residences and soon after that a small Methodist church, <u>the first Protestant church in Texas</u> was organized at Jonesborough in present-day Red River County.

Then in 1820 a <u>Baptist</u> preacher by the name of Joseph Bays camped on the American side of the Sabine River with other colonists who were gathering together to cross over and become Texas settlers. Bays ventured into Spanish Texas territory to preach at a private residence until he was ordered to stop by the authorities. But he must not have paid too much attention to those orders because three years later Rev. Bays was arrested at San Felipe for preaching again. However, they just couldn't hold onto this man of God and he escaped "somehow" while being transported to San Antonio for trial.

The big attraction that would now bring all the Protestant settlers into Texas was the Spanish land-grant idea that came to life in 1820. And there were a couple of other things that happened about that time that also helped bring them in. One of them was the fact that most folks believed that the United States would eventually buy eastern Texas from Mexico which would stimulate immigration and provide buyers for their land. So they were more than eager to come in and speculate on future land values.

The other attraction was that Mexico and the United States had no reciprocal agreements that enabled creditors to collect debts or to return fugitives. That made Texas a safe haven for <u>the</u>

many Mississippi Valley farmers who had defaulted on their loans when agricultural prices declined at the end of the War of 1812 and were besieged by bankers who were demanding immediate payment. Faced with seizure of their properties and even debtors' prison in some states, men loaded their families and belongings into wagons and headed for the Sabine River where creditors could not follow and there was opportunity to start over.

As it turned out though, there soon developed a religious issue to deal with. As we know, the legally mandated religion in the Texas territory was Catholicism while most of the Anglo-settlers coming in were Protestants. Beginning in 1824 when the Mexican Republic adopted its new constitution, each immigrant was required to take an oath of loyalty to the new nation and profess to be Christians. And since the Catholic Church was by law the only religion allowed, the oath implied that all these new settlers would become Catholics.

Even if the Protestant settlers had been willing to convert to Catholicism, the Catholic Church didn't send any priests into the area until 1831 which created a practical problem to deal with for folks wanting to get married: there was no legal provision for civil ceremonies and only Catholic priests had the authority to perform the nuptials. So finally, the settlers received permission from the authorities to sign a marriage bond, which had been a common practice in the back country of Virginia and the Carolinas before 1776, promising to formalize their unions when a Catholic priest next arrived into the area. Keep in mind that Protestant churches were not allowed in Texas until later on and pressure began to build for some changes to the Catholic-only law almost from the beginning of Mexico's great experiment for colonizing the territory with Anglo-American settlers.

As the infusion of land grant settlers intensified, some notable Protestant ministers came in with them even though the practice of their brand of Christianity was illegal. For example, Rev. Sumner Bacon, a pistol-packing Cumberland Presbyterian missionary, arrived in Texas in 1825. It was said that he preached wherever he could find worshipers, that he became an official agent of the American Bible Society in 1833 and that he eventually fought alongside Sam Houston in the revolution. A Cumberland Presbyterian church was organized in Red River County in 1833 as the first Presbyterian Church in Texas.

In 1829, Baptist preacher Rev. T.J. Pilgrim organized the first Sunday school in Texas at San Felipe. And about that same time, another one was established at Matagorda by Baptists from New York. But it was Rev. Daniel Parker, another Baptist preacher who is credited with establishing the first Baptist church in Texas and he did that by a clever interpretation of the Mexican law. His reasoning was that the ban on non-Catholic churches applied only to organizing new churches among folks who were already Texas residents but did not apply to previously organized churches whose members moved into the territory in mass as a congregation. So, he organized the *Pilgrim Church of Predestination Baptists* in Caldwell, Illinois, moved the whole group to Texas in 1833 and an initial congregation of 18 members held its first meetings in Austin colony in January 1834. And so, The Providence Church in Bastrop County in 1834 was <u>the first Baptist church organized in Texas</u>, and Rev. Moses Gage who served the church there was the first man licensed to preach in the territory. Historians have traced at least nine churches in East Texas that grew out of the efforts of the initial *Pilgrim* group.

And oh by the way, the oldest continuously operating Baptist Church in Texas today is the *Independence Baptist Church* located in Independence, Texas and operating since 1839. It just happens to be the church where Sam Houston was baptized on November 19, 1854. According to history when told after the baptism that his sins had been washed away, he famously remarked that he pitied the fish downstream.

As you might expect God was working behind the scenes to bring about His plans and purposes in amongst all this change that was going on. There were things that happened here and there that in looking back definitely facilitated the rise of Protestantism when it could have been a lot more difficult. For one thing many of the Mexican authorities were not so zealous in their enforcement of the prohibition against Protestant meetings. One famous example involved a meeting conducted in 1832 in Sabine County by Methodist minister Needham J. Alford and Presbyterian Sumner Bacon that was reported to <u>Col. José Piedras</u>, commander of the Mexican garrison at Nacogdoches. *"Are they stealing anything?"* Col. Piedras famously asked. *"Are they killing anybody? Are they doing anything bad?"* And since the answer to all those questions was *"No,"* he simply left the worshipers alone. And apparently the approach of Col. Piedras to this issue wasn't all that uncommon.

But there were other incidents where Mexican troops *<u>did</u>* operate more zealously than the example of Col. Piedras and there was a growing clamor of complaint among the settlers for more freedom of religion. In fact, the first sparks of the Texas Revolution flared in 1832 which just happened to "coincide" with something big going on back in Mexico City where internal rivalry had caused a series of leadership changes culminating in a takeover by none other than *<u>General Santa Ana</u>*. So all the Mexican troops that had been garrisoned in Texas to govern and keep order and prohibit the Protestant meetings left the northern territory and went back to Mexico to help establish the new government there leaving the Texas settlers pretty much to their own devices for a time.

While Anglo-American colonists continued to complain about a lack of religious freedom, the Mexican state government did finally liberalize the law as far as the national constitution allowed. The inevitable result of all this was an incoming flood of Protestant clergy and organizers that set the stage for the real Revolution that was to come in 1836.

The Effects of the Second Great Awakening

The Second Great Awakening occurred from 1790 to 1840 and it fundamentally altered the character of American religion. It is best known for its large camp meetings that were well suited to the frontier conditions of newly settled territories and helped lead large numbers of people to convert to Christianity.

Most evangelical churches of the day relied on itinerant preachers to reach far-flung areas where there were no established ministers. There were also important roles for lay people who took on major religious and administrative responsibilities within evangelical congregations and that included greater public roles for white women. And, of tremendous importance for the long term was that *The Second Great Awakening* encouraged and produced a much higher African-American participation in Christianity than ever before.

In sum, *The Second Great Awakening* marked a fundamental transition in American religious life by placing greater emphasis on human, God-given ability to change their situation for the better. By stressing that individuals could assert their "free will" in choosing to be saved and by suggesting that salvation was open to all human beings, *The Second Great Awakening* embraced a more optimistic view of things. The various outpourings that covered 50 years or so worked toward making the United States a much more deeply Protestant nation than it had been before and produced a "get-it-done" mentality for tens of thousands of settlers who went west to seek their fortunes. Those settlers knew what they wanted and were not afraid to go after it with all the gusto their Christian individualism had given them.

A Necessary Clarification

Now I wouldn't want to leave you with the impression that I think God's master plan for spreading Christianity in the New World necessarily favored Protestantism over Catholicism. It may seem that way but frankly, I'm just telling the story and I'm not sure how God looks at church denominations or how He evaluates what each one has adopted for their particular theology. I DO know that <u>no one group has all the answers</u> including the Methodists, the Baptists and the Presbyterians who were the first Protestant groups to come into Texas, and neither do the Catholics. God does things His way which is the one thing we can be sure of and the truth is God used both major groups, Catholic and Protestant alike at different times to bring His Word about faith in Christ to the New World.

Another thing we can be sure of according to Scripture is that Father God doesn't like it when people lose their right to freely choose especially under the New Testament. He doesn't like for one group to try to <u>force</u> their points of view on other folks in His Name because that's not the way He works. He has given us free will along with an *obligation* to choose between good and evil, and the mistake that Catholicism made in the western territories was to try to force people to adopt their ways of developing a relationship with Christ. What happened wasn't about one theology over another or Protestantism over Catholicism; it was about letting folks come to God through Christ and into His Kingdom the way they wanted to, and _if_ they wanted to, led by the Holy Spirit instead of legalism.

That's the way we are today: Catholic and Protestant living and working together with the freedom to choose the way we want to worship and the opportunity to be led by the Holy Spirit wherever He wants to go (Romans 8:14). Folks are also free to choose to reject God if they want to and be left to their own devices. It's our choice to make!

Freeman Smalley

T. J. Pilgrim

Daniel Parker

Needham J. Alford

Sumner Bacon

In 1815, Methodist William Stevenson (not pictured) began preaching in private residences. Soon after that a small Methodist church was organized at Jonesborough in present-day Red River County. It was the first Protestant church in Texas.

In the early 1820's two ardent Baptist evangelists, Freeman Smalley and Joseph Bays (not pictured) entered Texas in defiance of the Mexican Government ban on Protestantism. With few Catholic priests and a multitude of settlers, the Mexican Government was unable to enforce the ban so it was lifted in 1834. Prior to Texas Independence, only isolated individual preachers came to Texas.

In early January, 1829 Rev. T. J. Pilgrim arrived at San Felipe de Austin. When Stephen F. Austin and Pilgrim shook hands, a long friendship began as Pilgrim became interpreter and translator of Spanish documents for Austin's colony. He started a school known as Austin Academy with about forty students. Following that he organized the first Sunday School in Texas in the spring of 1829 with thirty-two pupils. But the Mexican government soon forced Pilgrim to close it.

Rev. Daniel Parker was the American leader in the *Primitive Baptist Church* in the Southern United States and the founder of numerous churches including *Pilgrim Primitive Baptist Church* at Elkhart, Texas. The *Pilgrim Predestinarian Regular Baptist Church* was constituted July 26, 1833 in Illinois and still exists today near Elkhart. Daniel Parker was one of the important frontier preachers in Texas leading in the organization of about nine churches in the eastern part of the state.

Pistol-packing Sumner Bacon arrived in Texas in 1825 as an unofficial Cumberland Presbyterian missionary. He preached where he could find worshipers, fought alongside Sam Houston in the revolution and became an official agent of the American Bible Society in 1833. With his Bibles protected by bearskins flung across his pack-horse's back, he is said to have distributed more than 2,000 of them, ignoring Mexican law, desperados, Indians and nature's elements. No wonder he needed a pistol!

The Providence Church in Bastrop County in 1834 was the first Baptist church organized in Texas and Moses Gage (not pictured) who served the church, was the first man licensed to preach in the territory.

GOD RELEASES PROTESTANT SETTLERS INTO THE TEXIAN TERRITORY:

<u>Below on the left</u> Stephen F. Austin's *Translation of the Laws, Orders, and Contracts, on Colonization ... San Filipe [sic] de Austin*: Printed by Godwin B. Cotten, 1829, this is the title page from the Texas Collection Library, The Center for American History.

The first book printed in Texas, this is Stephen F. Austin's account of the establishment of the first Anglo-American settlement of Texas and an English translation of the laws and documents relating to the founding of the colony.

And <u>on the right</u> is a copy of Stephen F. Austin's contract with the Mexican authorities to bring settlers into Texas and it is dated June 4, 1825. It has been called the most successful colonization deal in the history of America.

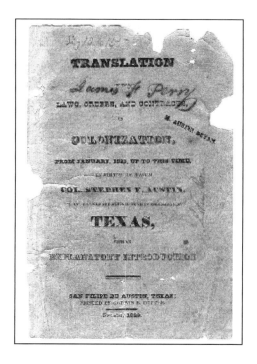

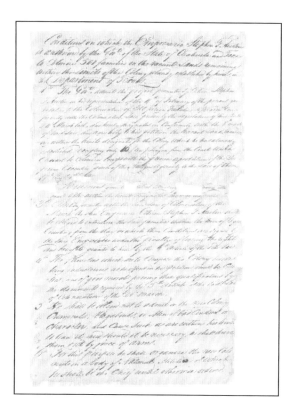

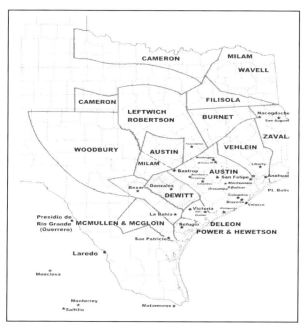

On the left the map of Impresario Grants for the Mexican State of Coahuila y Tejas during the period 1825-1832. Below s Texian flag.

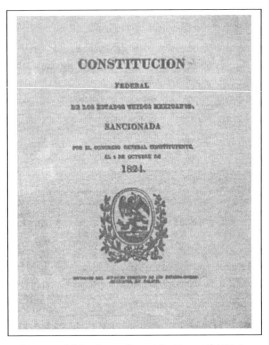

Cover of Mexican Constitution of 1824

Guadelupe Victoria
First President of the Republic of Mexico

This painting depicts settler rural life in early Texas around 1830. No condos yet.

A typical American Anglo family traveling by covered wagon to Texas during the 1830's where they had been promised a land grant upon presenting to the Mexican authorities there an appropriate *Character Certificate* stating that they were *"people of good moral habits and industry and a good citizen and friend to the laws and religion of the country.*

Five Uncommon Settlers

Now there are certain of the settlers in Texas history that have to be specially mentioned even though their names aren't usually brought up in a discussion about Christian influence. On the surface, these five famous men seemingly had little to do with religion but they <u>did</u> have a profound impact on Texas history and wound up changing the religious environment entirely.

They came to Texas with the great influx of settlers between 1820 and 1836, each one trying to sort out some special issues in his personal life, hoping to regain some lost ground and wanting to find a new life just like everybody else. No matter what happened in their lives before they came to Texas, they're remembered today as heroes, perhaps larger in death than they were in life although they were pretty big in life too. And one thing they did do, which maybe wasn't high on their personal list of priorities but happened anyway, was to help make a way for freedom of religion in what was to become the Republic of Texas.

Stephen F. Austin

Stephen Fuller Austin has been called the founder of Anglo-American Texas and eventually the *Father* of Texas. He was born in southwestern Virginia in 1793 and came to Texas in 1820 after his business failed in Missouri. He became the first of the "settler impresarios" when he contracted with the Mexican authorities to bring at least 300 families into Texas in 1821 in exchange for special land grants. He had complete civil and military authority over his colonists until 1828, subject only to nominal supervision from Mexican officials in San Antonio and Monterrey.

Austin's contemporaries largely disagreed with his rather cautious policy of continually conciliating those officials instead of standing up more strongly for their growing list of demands which of course included among other things the relaxation of the Catholic-only rule. The settlers accused him of weakness and instability but criticism didn't cause him to abandon his strategies. The fact is had he not taken this approach, rebellion would probably have erupted before the settlers were ready and set back independence for decades.

In 1834, Stephen F. Austin was finally able to arrange for a measure of religious tolerance with a new state law providing that no person should be molested on account of religious or political opinion if he didn't disturb public order. And, even though he had stubbornly opposed the growing call for revolution, Austin eventually supported the cause for a new republic when he saw that the revolution was inevitable. His support was a key step toward what was to soon follow and he became the first Secretary of State of the new republic. Unfortunately he soon died at age 43 on December 27, 1836.

Samuel Houston

Sam Houston was born on March 2, 1793 near Lexington, Virginia. From 1813 to 1814 he fought in the Creek War and was wounded at Horseshoe Bend. He was elected to the U.S. Congress in 1823 and again in 1825. In 1827 he became the governor of Tennessee. In 1832 after a failed marriage and a bit of a rough lifestyle, Houston moved to the Mexican territory of Texas where he was soon a prominent voice in pushing for secession from Mexico. As tensions mounted, Houston accepted an appointment to command a ragtag Texan army against the Mexican forces who were intent on putting down all rebellious elements.

Sam Houston though soon showed he was a brilliant military leader. After a series of small victories he was presented with a particular opportunity on April 21, 1836. Outnumbered by a better equipped Mexican army, Houston noticed that the Mexican General _Antonio López de Santa Anna_ had "for some reason" decided to split his forces. Seeing his chance Houston ordered the attack on the contingent at _San Jacinto_ and his decisive victory secured for Texas its independence in a matter of a couple of hours.

Sam Houston became the Texas George Washington. The city of Houston was named in his honor in 1836, and that same year the newly christened Lone Star Republic elected him as its president. After Texas joined the United States in 1845, Houston served as a U.S. Senator until 1860. Following the outbreak of the Civil War, Houston, who'd been elected governor of Texas, refused to pledge his allegiance to the Confederate States of America and an infuriated Texas legislature discharged him of his duties. He died on July 26, 1863 in Huntsville, Texas.

William B. Travis

William Barret Travis was the Texas commander at the battle of the _Alamo_. He was born in Saluda County, South Carolina on August 9, 1809 and came to Texas after abandoning his wife, son and unborn daughter in Claiborne, Alabama because he believed his wife had been unfaithful and that he was not the father of her unborn child. As the story goes, he killed a man over that situation and left for Texas where he arrived in 1831 as an illegal alien. He was illegal because the _Mexican Law of April 6, 1830_ among other things had specifically banned any further immigration of Anglo settlers into the Texas territory. But that didn't stop William B. Travis and he arrived in San Felipe de Austin and obtained land from impresario Stephen Austin.

He soon established a legal practice in Anahuac, a significant port of entry located on the eastern end of Galveston Bay. The purpose of the move there was to establish himself in an area where there were few attorneys while he learned Spanish the official language. From his base in Anahuac he traveled around the territory doing legal work and soon became associated with a group of militants who opposed the _Law of April 6, 1830_. Eventually this group became known as the _War Party_ as tensions increased between the Mexican government and American settlers.

Travis bounced around from skirmish to skirmish and was regarded by many Texans of the day as a trouble maker. Eventually he was branded an "outlaw" by the Mexican military authority in San Antonio. In January 1836 he accepted a commission as a lieutenant colonel in the Texas cavalry and became the chief recruiting officer for the Texas militia.

His appointment to that assignment soon took him to the Alamo the very next month where he died by a single gunshot to the head after a couple of days of fighting. As history would have it, the nature of Travis's death elevated him from a mere commander of an obscure garrison to a genuine hero of Texas and American history.

David Crockett

David Crockett was born in Greene County, East Tennessee on August 17, 1786. Between 1813 and 1821 he pursued a military career in various capacities and locations and was appointed or elected to several local township political positions. In August 1821 he took a big step up by running for a seat in the Tennessee legislature which he won. From that time forward he took an active interest in public land policy for the West. In 1827 he was elected to the U.S. House of Representatives, reelected in 1829 and proceeded to split with President Andrew Jackson and the Tennessee delegation on several issues including land reform and the Indian removal bill. In his 1831 campaign for a third term, Crockett openly and loudly attacked Jackson's policies and was defeated in a close election.

As David's fame grew he won reelection to Congress in 1833 but lost again in 1835 as his political split with Andrew Jackson grew deeper. Disenchanted with the political process and with his former constituents, David decided to do what he had famously threatened to do on several occasions: *"explore Texas and move his family there if the prospects were pleasing."* On November 1, 1835 he departed for the West with three other men and according to his statements he had no intention of getting into the fight for Texas independence. He arrived in Nacogdoches, Texas in early January 1836 and it didn't take long for the territory to change his mind about getting involved in the swiftly developing battle with Mexico.

The split with Andrew Jackson proved again to be a life-altering event because David made a fateful decision based on it. General Sam Houston had ordered William Travis to abandon the Alamo but Travis deliberately disregarded him. David had a decision to make when he got to San Antonio: he could either join up with General Houston or with Travis in the Alamo. Sam Houston was an Andrew Jackson supporter so David Crockett chose to go to the Alamo. And of course along with many other heroes, he died there on March 6, 1836 after living in Texas for a total of two months: short time, big impact.

James Bowie

James Bowie was born in Logan County, Kentucky on March 10, 1796 and became a well-known pioneer, soldier, smuggler, slave trader, and land speculator. Like many frontiersmen of the day, Bowie became intrigued by the idea of Texas, so he moved here in 1830 apparently one step ahead of his creditors back in Louisiana. In short order he found plenty to keep him busy including: 1) a land speculation scheme, 2) a victorious defense against a Tawakoni Indian attack while 3) looking for a particular silver mine he had heard about and 4) the charms of the Senorita *Ursula Veramendi*, the well-connected daughter of the mayor/vice governor of San Antonio. His fame and reputation as a tough frontiersman grew rapidly and in 1831 he married Ursula and took up residence in San Antonio. Unfortunately, she and her parents soon died tragically of cholera.

In the following years Bowie became actively involved in the independence movement and was responsible for several skirmish victories. But ultimately, to make a long story short, he made the bad decision to also disobey Sam Houston's orders to demolish and abandon the old Alamo Mission in San Antonio and sought instead to fortify it and make a defense. After all, San Antonio had become his home town. When William Travis eventually arrived on the scene, there was strife between the two over which of them would lead the fortification. But David Crockett the experienced politician soon arrived and was able to diffuse things helped by the fact that Bowie became debilitated by a sudden illness. History says that James Bowie was killed on his sick pallet firing his pistols at the enemy when the Mexican army overran the Alamo on March 6, 1836.

James Bowie was another of the rough and tumble settlers that came to Texas to seek their destinies. He came here with his Bowie knife in hand, the same one he first used in 1827 to kill a rival, and he became in death an unlikely hero, one of the five special heroes that have captured the imagination of succeeding generations of Texans since that day in the Alamo. *"Remember the Alamo"* became the war-cry for the Texas army that attacked Santa Ana at *San Jacinto* and won the independence from Mexico the settlers had wanted. These were five special settlers that will never be forgotten and the independence they helped win produced freedom of religion for the people of Texas.

FIVE EXTRAORDINARY SETTLERS IN THE HISTORY OF TEXAS:

Stephen F. Austin

Samuel Houston

Col. William B. Travis

David (not Davy) Crockett

Jim Bowie

Part Six:
The Republicans

On March 2, 1836 the *Texas Declaration of Independence* was signed by the sixty members of the *Convention of 1836* held at Washington-on-the-Brazos and a new country was born called the *Republic of Texas*. People who live in a Republic can be called REPUBLICANS so the title of this article is not about the current-day GOP political party. It's about the thousands of settlers who suddenly found themselves moving from the jurisdiction of one country to another, from Mexico to the Republic of Texas. Of the sixty men who signed the *Declaration* only ten had lived in Texas more than six years, some fifteen of them had been here for less than a year. And, most of the delegates were members of the *War Party* and had already decided as they arrived at the Convention that Texas should declare its independence from Mexico.

The convention actually started on March 1 and the delegates soon selected a committee of five to draft a *Declaration of Independence*. The committee was led by George Childress and included Edward Conrad, James Gaines, Bailey Hardeman, and Collin McKinney. Somehow they were able to submit their draft back to the main group in only 24 hours leading historians to the conclusion that Childress had probably written down most of it before he arrived at the Convention. And of course there had been other meetings and conventions over the previous five years when independence had been discussed and written about before being set aside and tabled for future discussion. So the *Convention of 1836* assembled with one principal purpose in mind which was to put into action what the *War Party* had already been discussing and working on for quite some time.

Consider for a moment that the relationship with Mexico had come to all out revolution in a mere fifteen years. The main influx of English-speaking Anglo-Protestant settlers had started arriving in Texas in 1820-21 in response to the original Spanish land grant idea that was quickly followed by the Mexican version of that same program a year later when they won their independence from Spain. As we've seen in previous articles, the Spanish and Mexican authorities had originally wanted the settlers to come in to help develop the territory and secure the northern borders, but almost from the beginning the settlers were quite "unsettled" about life under Mexican control and soon began to voice their opposition to a number of issues that were interfering with the *"life, liberty and pursuit of happiness"* idea they had been used to when they lived in the U.S.

Among other things, the *Texas Declaration of Independence* mentions the following principal reasons for wanting to separate from Mexico:

- The 1824 Constitution establishing Mexico as a federal republic had been changed into a military dictatorship by Gen. Antonio López de Santa Anna.

- The Mexican government had invited settlers to Texas and promised them constitutional liberty and republican government but had then reneged on those guarantees.

- Texas was a part of the Mexican state of Coahuila, known as *Coahuila y Tejas*, with the capital in the far-distant city of Saltillo, Mexico and as a result the affairs of Texas were decided too far away from the territory. And, they were conducted in the Spanish language instead of English.

- Political rights that the settlers had previously been accustomed to such as the right to keep and bear arms and the right to trial by jury were being denied.

- No system of public education had been established.

- The settlers were not allowed freedom of religion.

Now the settlers had been complaining about these things for quite a while leading up to March 2, 1836 but they hadn't gotten anywhere. The fact is, all their complaining and agitating had actually gotten additional immigration officially suspended by the *Mexican Law of April 6, 1830* which only led to more complaining and resistance. The Law didn't really slow down immigration all that much but it did provide more fuel for the fire of resistance. As tensions grew during the following five years, there were some <u>major</u> events to be pointed out that culminated in the *Convention of 1836.*

April 6, 1830 – Relations between the Texas settlers and Mexico City reached a low point when Mexico banned any further Immigration into Texas by settlers from the U.S.

June 26, 1832 – The Battle of Velasco resulted in the first casualties in Texas' relationship with Mexico. After several days of fighting, the Mexicans under Domingo de Ugartechea were forced to surrender when they ran out of ammunition.

1832–1833 – The Convention of 1832 and the Convention of 1833 both instigated by the *War Party* were triggered by growing dissatisfaction among the Anglo settlers with the policies of the Mexican government.

October 2 1835 – Texans repulsed a detachment of Mexican cavalry at the *Battle of Gonzales* and the revolution began.
October 9, 1835 – The *Goliad Campaign of 1835* ended when George Collingsworth, Ben Milam, and forty-nine other Texans stormed the presidio at Goliad and defeated a small detachment of Mexican defenders.

October 28, 1835 – Jim Bowie, James Fannin and 90 Texans defeated 450 Mexican troops at the Battle of Concepcion near San Antonio.

November 3, 1835 – The Consultation (basically another Convention) met to consider options for more autonomous rule for Texas. A document known as the *Organic Law* outlined the organization and functions of a new provisional government.

November 8, 1835 – The *Grass Fight* near San Antonio was won by the Texans under Jim Bowie and Ed Burleson.

December 11, 1835 – Mexican troops under Gen. Cos surrendered San Antonio to the Texans following the Siege of Bexar. Ben Milam was killed during the extended siege.

Up until this point things seemed to be going for the Texans leading to the *Convention of 1836* and the Texas settlers were in a victorious frame of mind at the end of 1835. But things were about to get a lot rougher.

February 23, 1836 – On this date approximately 1,500 Mexican soldiers marched into the city of San Antonio as the first step in a campaign to retake Texas. For the next 10 days the two armies engaged in several skirmishes with minimal casualties. Aware that his garrison called the *Alamo* could not withstand an attack by such a large force, Travis wrote multiple letters pleading for more men and supplies, but fewer than 100 reinforcements actually arrived. Numbers vary but at least 183 to 186 Texans in the Alamo were holding off the Mexican troops.

March 6 1836 – Texans under commanding officer Col. William B. Travis were overwhelmed by the Mexican army at the <u>*Battle of the Alamo*</u> during the third of three assaults carried out that day. The Texans had repulsed the invading army on the first two tries but were not able to make it through the third. All of the Texans perished except for a few locals that were released to tell the tale of the Mexican "invincibility." It should be remembered that among those who died at the Alamo were William Garnett and James Northcross, Baptist and Methodist ministers respectively. Also, historians estimate that at least 600 Mexican troops were either killed or wounded.

There were two reactions to this military disaster. Many Texans went immediately to join the Texas army under General Sam Houston to defend their new country. On March 6, 1836 when the Alamo fell, the Republic of Texas was only four days old. A number of other Texans though were caught in the path of the advancing Mexican army and fled for their lives. But immediately the rallying cry of *"Remember the Alamo"* became an inspiration to those in the Army of Texas as they fought for independence.

March 10, 1836 -- Sam Houston abandoned Gonzales in a general retreat eastward to avoid the invading Mexican army.

March 27, 1836 -- James Fannin and nearly 400 Texans were executed by the Mexicans at the *Goliad Massacre* under the order of General Santa Anna. "Remember Goliad" became another rallying cry for the Texas army.

April 21, 1836 -- Texans under General Sam Houston routed the Mexican forces of Santa Anna at the *Battle of San Jacinto*. Thus, independence was won in one of the most decisive military battles in world history. In fact, the Texans actually took Santa Anna prisoner after the battle and the Mexican general and dictator of Mexico <u>bought his freedom by signing a treaty recognizing Texas independence</u> which he later disavowed.

Religious Freedom in the Republic

Now when most folks think about the battle for independence in Texas, they tend to overlook the part that religion played. Yes, Texans were concerned about their political rights and they felt they were being unfairly governed by a dictator far away in Mexico City who spoke a different language. And yes, the way of life that the Mexican government had attempted to impose on all the settlers was a big change from what they had been accustomed to in the U.S.

But underlying all of that was the religious aspect. By law Texans were supposed to exclusively observe the Catholic faith. But there were few if any Priests who were available around the territory to provide ministry. Almost all of the settlers were Protestant Christians who before they came to Texas had known how to find a church or a circuit rider that spoke English when they needed ministry. In Texas they weren't able to find a Catholic minister most of the time and if they did find one, the ministry was usually in Spanish. A soul once saved cannot go indefinitely without spiritual food and while secular historians have tended to drop this subject to lower levels on the list of priorities for these settlers, the truth is Christian people are compelled to seek knowledgeable teaching and reassurance to help strengthen their faith. Why do you think the Protestant circuit riders, evangelists and missionaries had been so much in demand *before* the Revolution? Why did they risk arrest and jail time to come across the border and minister to all the new settlers? Christianity was important and the right to free choice was paramount. And oh by the way: the previously discussed *Second Great Awakening* was an ongoing catalyst that was encouraging circuit riders, ministers and settlers alike to go into the new territory in search of a new life at the very time that independence from Mexico was being sought after.

Many people don't realize that the *Texas Declaration of Independence* dealt specifically with the question of religious freedom. The *Declaration* is actually a list of complaints against the government of Mexico and after listing all the complaints, it declares independence to be the inevitable and only remedy for all the suffering the people of Texas had been forced to endure.

The sixteenth paragraph or complaint of the *Texas Declaration of Independence* reads as follows:

It (the Mexican Government) denies us the right of worshipping the Almighty to the dictates of our own conscience, by the support of a national religion, calculated to promote the temporal interests of its human functionaries, rather than the glory of the true and living God.

So, one of the important things that happened on March 2, 1836 and confirmed at the *Battle of San Jacinto* was that the people of Texas won religious freedom for themselves. If they wanted to worship as Protestants and in the English language they could. If they preferred Catholicism and/or the Spanish language they could choose to worship that way too. So could people of other religions come and settle in the new Republic with a free choice: they could choose to stay in their traditional religions or they were free according to the new law of the land to choose whatever religion they wanted to. Or they could choose to have no religion.

For some reason secular historians want to make a big deal out of the fact that at the beginning of the Republic only about one settler in eight was "affiliated with a church" as if those early Republicans weren't religious or were no longer interested in the Christianity they had left behind in the U.S. Nothing could be further from the truth and you can speculate for yourself about why secular folks insist on leaving this impression. Would it not be more logical to conclude that the reason why only one-eighth of the population was involved with a church was that there were so few established churches in the territory, or that those few churches were often great distances apart across territory that was occupied by hostiles, or that Texas was largely a rural population or that they had just come out of a Catholic dictatorship where Protestant ministers were routinely arrested, jailed and deported? Does it make any sense that seven-eighths of the people who settled in Texas were unchurched non-believers contrary to the demographics of the country they were coming out of after thirty-five years of *The Second Great Awakening*? Did the *Texas Declaration of Independence* not clearly and sufficiently articulate a deep-seated desire of the settlers for freedom of religion so they could worship openly and freely however they wanted to?

The truth is, just as soon as the Republic was formed and freedom of religion declared, there was an explosion of Protestant ministry into the territory. And people responded to the new availability of ministry. They had been waiting for it...<u>and all along they had been agitating for it</u>. The settlers who had been Protestant Christians before they came into the Territory didn't lose their Christianity after they immigrated and then suddenly regain it again after independence. Secular thinking can dream up such a circular process but true Christianity just doesn't work that way. Indeed ministers came across the border illegally during the last fifteen years of Mexican control because they were in demand. They came because they were needed by God-fearing Christians who had emigrated from America.

Once the turmoil of the Texas Revolution receded, the major church denominations were finally able to take a serious interest in missionary work in the new Republic. The first official Methodist missionaries came in 1837 when Martin Ruter, Littleton Fowler and Robert Alexander were named by the Missionary Society of the Methodist Episcopal Church of the United States. Ruter who was the superintendent of the mission activity lived only six months after coming to Texas. However, his influence on Texas education lasted long after his death

.

Ruter divided Texas into three circuits. Circuit riders fanned out through the Republic led by Ruter who covered more than 2,200 miles on horseback during his short service. These ministers visited neighborhoods, determined whether the people wanted a worship service and if so they provided one. When sufficient interest was demonstrated, a church was organized. By 1839, there were 20 Methodist churches with 350 members in Texas. Two years later the aggressive Methodists had enlarged that number to 1,878 members. The first separate Methodist conference for Texas was authorized in 1840 and organized by Bishop Beverly Waugh.

James Huckins was the first official Baptist missionary and was appointed by the Home Missionary Society in 1840. After his arrival he asked for 15 missionaries to help cover the large, sparsely settled territory.

The mission board of the General Presbyterian Assembly appointed Rev. W.C. Blair missionary to Texas in 1839 and located him in Victoria. A decade later, the Presbyterian Church U.S.A. showed 10 ministers, 15 churches and 329 members in the state.

The first Episcopal services were held at Matagorda on Christmas Day in 1838, and the first parish was organized a month later. Episcopal churches were also established in Houston and Galveston in 1838 and 1839.

The Roman Catholic Church, which had been in dire straits after years of neglect, began rebuilding in 1838. Texas was placed under the authority of the Bishop Antoine Blanc of New Orleans. Rev. John Timon and Rev. Juan Francisco Llebaría, both priests of the Vincentian order whose American headquarters was in Missouri, were sent to the new republic to determine the state of the church. They got no farther than Houston, where they gathered information from around the Republic. Poor roads, bad weather and Indians kept the priests from touring the rest of the new republic. In 1842 Father Jean Marie Odin, a Vincentian from France, was named Vicar Apostolic of Texas to continue the work of rebuilding that Father Timon started. By 1846, 10 churches or chapels were completed. The Diocese of Galveston was erected in 1847 and included the new state of Texas, and Father Odin was named its first bishop.

In sum, during the time of the Republic the Body of Christ began to make up for lost time and made rapid strides. Circuit riders faithfully carried the message of virtually every church denomination across the sparsely inhabited territory. Bad weather, a lack of roads, sickness and hostile Indians were constant challenges. Their courage and dedication were similar to that of the Roman Catholic Franciscans who had first faced the fierce Indian tribes and both groups, Protestant and Catholic alike, contributed martyrs to the evangelical efforts in the Texas territory. The point is though, as soon as the legal barriers went down, missionaries and ministers were ready and came into the Republic to start a great work. But even while the Church was on the move, there was in the forefront a difficult political climate that would carry the new country into a future of rapid change.

Politics in the Republic

Texas was a sovereign independent Republic for more than nine years: from March 2, 1836 until December 29, 1845. During that first year, Stephen F. Austin known as the *Father of Texas* died on December 27 after serving only two months as Secretary of State and five different sites served as temporary capitals of Texas: Washington-on-the-Brazos, Harrisburg, Galveston, Velasco and Columbia before President Sam Houston moved the capital to Houston in 1837. In 1839 the capital was finally moved to the new town of Austin by the next president, Mirabeau B. Lamar.

The first Congress of the Republic of Texas convened in October 1836 at Columbia (now called West Columbia). As the new Republic started off internal politics involved a confrontation between two main factions. A *nationalist* group led by Mirabeau B. Lamar advocated the continued independence of Texas, the expulsion of all Native Americans, and the expansion of Texas to the Pacific Ocean. Their opponents led by Sam Houston advocated the annexation of Texas to the United States and peaceful co-existence with Native Americans. Obviously the Sam Houston school of thought eventually prevailed but at that first Congress a key decision was made that would greatly affect the future of Texas: it overturned the Mexican prohibition of slavery.

Although Texas was doing well enough governing itself, Mexico refused to recognize its independence even though President Santa Ana had signed a Peace Treaty recognizing Texas independence after the *Battle of San Jacinto*. Nevertheless, on March 5, 1842 a Mexican force of more than 500 troops led by <u>Ráfael Vásquez</u> invaded Texas for the first time since the revolution. They soon headed back to the Rio Grande after briefly occupying San Antonio. Soon after that though, a bigger force of some 1,400 Mexican troops under the command of the French mercenary general Adrian Woll launched a second attack and captured San Antonio on September 11, 1842. A Texas militia retaliated at the *Battle of Salado Creek*. However on September 18, the militia was defeated by Mexican soldiers and Texas Cherokee Indians during the Dawson Massacre. Eventually though the Mexican army retreated from San Antonio and went back to Mexico.

Mexico's attacks on Texas intensified the conflict between the two political factions and produced an incident known as the *Texas Archive War*. In order to "protect" the Texas national archives, President Sam Houston ordered them out of Austin. Austin residents were suspicious of the president's motives because Houston didn't much care for the capital being there and at gunpoint they forced the archives to be brought back to Austin. The Texas Congress criticized President Houston for the incident and the whole thing actually served to solidify Austin as Texas's capital for the Republic and on into the future. Politics are politics after all, no matter the century they're being played in.

All during the Republic there was concern about the Mexican threat and the fact that the funds available to provide the related defense and protection were quite limited. As time went on the idea of being annexed by the U.S. grew in popularity in Texas but at first it was rejected by the U.S. because Texas had allowed slavery to come in and the U.S. didn't want another slave state. So Texas politicians then considered some kind of an arrangement of protection with either England or France, and the U.S. liked that idea even less than slavery which finally led to U.S. annexation in 1845. Being independent was the dream of many idealists and lovers of Texas but reality was on the horizon because Texas needed some help to protect itself, to establish financial credibility and achieve its destiny. And help was on the way.

The Texas Constitution   Copy of Original Constitution

On the frozen morning of March 1, 1836, forty-five men shivered in an unfinished house in the tiny hamlet of Washington, Texas. They and fifteen other men who later joined them, representing all the municipalities in the Mexican province of Texas, declared the province to be a free and independent republic. At the time of their meeting the Alamo was already under siege and would fall in five days.

Commandancy of the Alamo
Bejar, Feby. 24, 1836

To the People of Texas & All Americans in the World

Fellow citizens & compatriots

I am besieged, by a thousand or more of the Mexicans under Santa Anna I have sustained a continual Bombardment & cannonade for 24 hours & have not lost a man The enemy has demanded a surrender at discretion, otherwise, the garrison are to be put to the sword, if the fort is taken I have answered the demand with a cannon shot, & our flag still waves proudly from the walls I shall never surrender or retreat. Then, I call on you in the name of Liberty, of patriotism & everything dear to the American character, to come to our aid, with all dispatch The enemy is receiving reinforcements daily & will no doubt increase to three or four thousand in four or five days. If this call is neglected, I am determined to sustain myself as long as possible & die like a soldier who never forgets what is due to his own honor & that of his country VICTORY OR DEATH.

William Barret Travis,
Lt. Col. comdt.

P.S. The Lord is on our side. When the enemy appeared in sight we had not three bushels of corn. We have since found in deserted houses 80 or 90 bushels and got into the walls 20 or 30 head of Beeves. Travis

Typed copy of the famous appeal letter from Col. William Travis when he found his garrison surrounded and hopelessly outnumbered. They held out for 10 more days.

When the Texian garrison in the Alamo was defeated on March 6, 1836 the official newspaper of the Mexican government called the *Diario del Gobierno* celebrated the bravery and success of Mexican officers and soldiers in achieving what was described as a complete and brilliant victory. "Long Live the Mexican Republic!" proclaimed the headlines. "Long live *General Santa Anna* and the brave army, victors of the Fort of the Alamo in Texas!" The Texian response was simply: "Remember the Alamo!

On April 21, 1836 one of the most decisive battles in world history was fought at San Jacinto located outside of La Porte, Texas. The two armies were led by a couple of famous people:

General Santa Ana

General Sam Houston

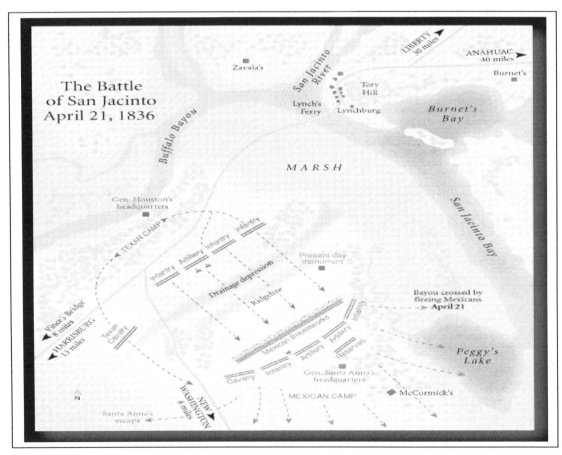

The battle was waged as shown on this map. You can visit this site today and see firsthand where the great battle was fought. The Mexican Army was defeated in only 20 minutes.

This famous painting shows the wounded General Sam Houston reclined under a tree receiving the surrender of the Mexican General Santa Anna as the new republic suddenly became viable.

This little building is an exact replica of the 1836 Texas Capital Building in West Columbia, Texas

SOME OF THE MAIN LEADERS OF THE BODY OF CHRIST IN THE NEW REPUBLIC:

Martin Ruter
(Methodist)

James Huckins
(Baptist)

Sumner Bacon
(Cumberland Presbyterian)

Bishop Antoine Blanc
(Catholic)

Rev. John Timon
(Catholic)

On June 21, 1837 Martin Ruter accepted a Methodist missionary assignment in Texas and has been called the spiritual father of Texas. Exhausted, Ruter died of fever May 16, 1838.

Rev. James Huckins became the first Southern Baptist missionary to Texas in 1840 and eventually became founder and pastor of two Baptist churches in Galveston and Houston.

Sumner Bacon is pictured again here because of his direct involvement in the Republic. Indeed, he served as a chaplain and courier for **Gen. Sam Houston** carrying dispatches to the Alamo, Goliad, and Victoria. He also traveled to New Orleans for gunpowder. In 1836 he organized the first Cumberland Presbyterian church in Texas near San Augustine and in 1837 helped start from his home the Texas Presbytery.

The Roman Catholic Church was in dire straits after years of neglect and began rebuilding in 1838. Texas was placed under the authority of Bishop Antoine Blanc of New Orleans. Rev. John Timon was sent to the new republic to determine the state of the church and in July 1840 was named Prefect Apostolic of the Republic of Texas.

In the fall of 1844, the Texas Baptist Education Society petitioned the Congress of the Republic of Texas to charter a Baptist university. Republic President Anson Jones signed the Act of Congress on February 1, 1845, officially establishing Baylor University named after one of its sponsors Judge R. E. B. Baylor.

THE FLAGS OF THE REPUBLIC:

Texas Navy Flag

In November of 1835 the *General Council of Texas* commissioned the Republic of Texas Navy. The flag of the Texas Navy was created by Charles Hawkins who was later appointed as the first Commodore of the Navy. The new Navy participated in a failed expedition to capture Tampico but the small force was quickly captured and almost all of the men were executed. Somehow only the two leaders of the group managed to escape.

First Lone Star Texas Flag

The first Lone Star Flag of Texas was created by Sarah Dodson for her husband Archelaus, a member of the Texas Volunteers. Archelaus's company marched under the Dodson Flag to San Antonio and they fought under this flag during the siege of San Antonio and the Texian's capture of the Alamo.

Second "National Flag" of the Republic of Texas

In December 1836 the new Government approved the recommendation of President David Burnett for a new design for the "National Flag" of Texas. Some were made with gold stars, others had white stars. Little consideration was given to the previous National Flag design adopted only eight months earlier. This flag represented the theme of Texas as an independent nation that was getting on with the business of building the country instead of fomenting confrontation. On March 3, 1837 the Republic of Texas under this flag was recognized by the United States as an independent nation.

Once independence finally happened support began to grow for a new flag and
in 1839 the flag that we now associate with Texas was designed and approved. The
flag maintained its lone star and serves as a banner and symbol for the state to this day.

Part Seven:
The Americans

In this article we'll be dealing with the difficult twenty-nine year period of Texas history from 1845 until 1874 that started out with great expectations but ended up instead in great trial and adversity. As you already know, Texas was a sovereign independent Republic for almost ten years: from March 2, 1836 until December 29, 1845. The end of the Republic came when U.S. President James K. Polk took office on March 4, 1845 and followed through on a campaign promise by endorsing the previously passed congressional annexation legislation sponsored by President John Tyler and then encouraging the government of Texas to accept the U.S. invitation. It took almost the rest of the year for Texas to draw up a new state constitution and complete the ratification process and the invitation was officially accepted on December 29, 1845. Once again by the stroke of a pen, Texans moved from one country to another. Suddenly all those *Texian* settlers were Americans but most of them had been Americans before they immigrated to Texas so they pretty much knew what to expect.

By 1830 the aggregate population of Texas had been about 20,000 which grew to an estimated 75,000 by 1840 according to the U.S. Census Bureau. By 1850 it had grown to 210, 000 as the full effect of freedom of religion and annexation to the U. S. took effect and that went to 720,000 by the 1860 Census and 819,000 by 1870 which is the last Census we're looking at in this series of articles so we can still call the period that we've been studying "early" Texas. In the short span of only 40 years, the place that had been so hard to colonize for more than three hundred years was finally experiencing a population explosion that goes on to the current day. Texas has indeed flourished as a part of the United States of America.

But the history of Texas in the U.S. is divided into two periods. The first one lasted from the Annexation on December 29, 1845 until Texas seceded from the Union and became independent again on February 1, 1861 followed closely by joining the Confederate States of America on March 2, 1861. Then at the end of the Civil War, Texas became a defeated *possession* of the United States on June 19, 1865 but it was not officially readmitted until March 30, 1870 thus to begin the second period of statehood. Texas was the next to the last Confederate state to be readmitted; Georgia was the last. Even after it was officially readmitted, Texas would have to endure four more years of Reconstruction, a total of nine years before things could get back to "normal" statehood.

Annexing Texas in the first place was not an easy proposition because Texas was a vast slave-holding territory and the idea of bringing another slave state into the Union wasn't totally popular, except of course among the existing slave states. The fact is Texas had applied for statehood previously and had been turned down over the slave issue. But when it became necessary for the Texas Republic to petition England for assistance in dealing with Mexican hostility, President John Tyler pulled off a political "miracle" with the U. S. Congress to get their approval for annexation. In doing that he used up pretty much all of his remaining political capital and had to give up his quest for re-election in 1844. As an independent candidate he didn't have a lot of political capital anyway, but somehow nearing the end of his presidency he was able to get the annexation bill through both houses of Congress and obtain a commitment from the Democrat candidate President James K. Polk to sign the bill once he took office.

Even though the slave-holding aspect of the annexation was politically difficult, the idea of adding a new state and expanding the territory of the U. S. was a popular idea. In the end, Polk's narrow victory in the election of November 1844 over his Whig opponent Henry Clay has been attributed by historians to the popular view of expansion and Manifest Destiny. Henry Clay and the Whigs generally were strongly opposed to adding another slave state and were viewed as being anti-expansion. And so, Texas came into the Union as the 28th state after a huge political battle expecting U.S. protection from Mexican harassment. It also needed some economic help after 10 years of having to defend itself against the ongoing armed conflicts. Mexico had already officially severed diplomatic relations with the U. S. on March 28, 1845 when the final annexation process started and as that process was being finalized, the U.S. was preparing to send troops to defend its new southern border.

The only problem with that was there was a big disagreement on where that southern border of Texas actually was. As you might expect from politicians, the annexation bill failed to specify anything on that particular question so the U. S. decided it should be the Rio Grande River since Texas had always told folks that that's where it was. And before you know it, the U. S. was sending troops down there to establish it at the Rio Grande even while Mexico was saying that the southern border had always been the Nueces River some distance to the north. So from the get-go there was a border dispute of major proportions.

The U. S. sent diplomats down to Mexico City to try to negotiate the dispute and even offered to pay Mexico 25 million dollars for the disputed area. But that was a really, really unpopular idea down there and the Mexican army even wanted to depose their President *José Joaquín de Herrera* just for thinking about taking the money. After that, the U. S. perspective was that the next Mexican incursion across the Rio Grande River was an invasion into its new state and would be an act of war.

President John Tyler

Henry Clay

President James K. Polk

US President John Tyler, champion of Texas annexation said: "Texas was the great scheme that occupied me." He initiated complicated political measures in a divided Congress to win annexation even though he had to withdraw from his re-election race of 1844 to get it done.

Henry Clay leader of the Whig Party opposed the annexation of Texas based on the argument that it posed a danger to the *integrity of the Union*. He was vividly aware of the divisiveness of the slavery issue on a national level and was narrowly defeated by Polk in 1844.

James K. Polk of Tennessee is pictured here as president-elect of the United States during the joint house Texas treaty debates. He implemented annexation as soon as he took office.

Anson Jones
Last president of the Republic of Texas

James Pinckney Henderson
First Governor of the State of Texas

The Mexican-American War 1846-1848

And war _did_ come soon after the annexation. American troops had been stationed to the south along the Rio Grande River to turn back any Mexican invasions and soon enough on April 25, 1846 a large contingent of Mexican cavalry attacked an American patrol in that disputed area between the Rio Grande and Nueces rivers killing 16 Americans. Then on May 3 Mexican troops initiated a siege of Fort Texas. On May 8, General Zachary Taylor led 2,500 U.S. troops to relieve the fort and the Mexican soldiers retreated.

That was enough for President Polk, and the U.S. Congress officially declared war against Mexico on May 13, 1846 with Mexico returning the favor to the U.S. on July 7. Throughout the official hostilities, the U.S. maintained two fronts: one in the Mexican interior south of the Rio Grande River and one in California. There was no further fighting in the new state of Texas. But guess who was in command of the Mexican forces that were organized to oppose the U.S. troops! You're right: it was that old nemesis _Generalisimo_ Santa Anna who was again in command of the Mexican army.

Following its two-front plan, the U. S. sent the part of its army already on the Rio Grande River under General Taylor to invade Mexico while a second force under Colonel Stephen Kearny was sent to occupy New Mexico and California. Kearny's campaign into New Mexico and California encountered little resistance and the residents of both territories accepted American occupation with minimum reaction. Meanwhile, General Taylor's army fought several battles south of the Rio Grande, captured the important city of Monterrey and defeated a major Mexican force at the Battle of Buena Vista in February 1847.

But Taylor wasn't too enthusiastic about making a further major invasion into Mexico, and on several occasions he failed to pursue the Mexican Army aggressively after defeating it. In apparent great disgust with Taylor's reluctance, President Polk revised his war strategy and ordered General Winfield Scott to take an army by sea to Veracruz, capture that key seaport and march inland to Mexico City. A large contingent of Taylor's troops was transferred over to General Scott who took Veracruz in March 1847 and then began a march to Mexico City. Despite the Mexican resistance, Scott's campaign was marked by an unbroken series of victories and he entered Mexico City on September 14, 1847. The fall of the Mexican capital ended the military phase of the war and peace for Texas was finally secure.

On February 2, 1848 negotiations in Mexico City on the development of the _Treaty of Guadalupe Hidalgo_ were completed and subsequently ratified by the national congresses of both countries. Mexico ceded to the United States nearly all the territory now included in the states of New Mexico, Utah, Nevada, Arizona, California, Texas, and western Colorado for a payment of 15 million dollars and the U.S. assumed part of its citizens' claims against Mexico up to 3.5 million dollars. Zachary Taylor became a national hero and succeeded Polk as president in 1849 and General Winfield Scott became another hero and the longest serving General in U.S. history.

In war the victors are always happy for a few minutes but there are negative consequences of them that last for generations. In Mexico this particular war discredited the conservatives and left a stunned and despondent country behind. It also reinforced the worst stereotypes that each country held about the other and the restoration of relations after the war proceeded quite slowly. The truth is too that resentments within the cultures of both Texas and Mexico have simmered now for more than 150 years and both sides have had to rise above their feelings to seek their respective destinies among the nations of the world and in the Kingdom of God.

The Mexican–American war and the annexation of Texas just before it also served to highlight the slavery issue, which according to historians had been largely dormant since the *Missouri Compromise of 1820*. On August 8, 1846, Representative David Wilmot of Pennsylvania tried to add an amendment to a treaty appropriations bill banning slavery from any territory acquired from Mexico but it was never passed. It *did* lead though to quite a bit of spirited debate and contributed greatly to increased tensions around the country. The status of slavery in the newly acquired territories was eventually temporarily defused by the *Compromise of 1850*, but only after the nation had come dangerously close to civil war. In sum, the annexation of Texas had exposed a serious division in America that only eleven years later would produce the greatest crisis and the greatest loss of life the United States has ever had to deal with.

The Mexican maps of the day back in 1845 showed the Republic of Texas to be the smaller area to the right in the map on the left following along the Nueces River to the south instead of the Rio Grande River to the further south. But the Republic of Texas claimed the entire area shown by the map on the right and was annexed by the U.S. with the understanding that it was this larger area to the right that was being annexed. The result of this disagreement turned out to be the Mexican-American War.

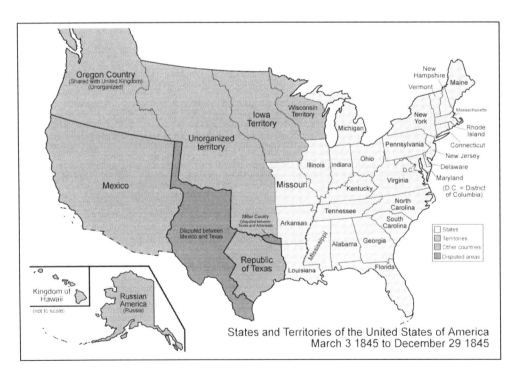

This is what the U.S. map looked like at the end of 1845 when Texas was finally annexed including that disputed territory to the left of the area labeled the Republic of Texas. At the end of the Mexican-American War in 1848, all of the western territory labeled Mexico was ceded to the U.S. for a payment of 15 million dollars plus 3.5 million dollars to cover settler claims against Mexico.

Gen. Zachary Taylor

Gen. Winfield Scott

President Santa Anna

Two new faces confront a familiar one from the past...

Zachary Taylor was a career officer in the United States Army, rising to the rank of major general. His status as a national hero as a result of his victories in the Mexican-American War won him election to the White House despite his vague political beliefs.

General Winfield Scott, known as "Old Fuss and Feathers" and the "Grand Old Man of the Army," served on active duty as a general longer than any other man in American history. Many historians rate him the best American commander of his time. He became a national hero after his victories in the Mexican-American War and serving for a time as military governor of Mexico City.

As soon as American forces entered Mexico City, President Santa Anna decided to make another treaty and encourage the Americans to go home. He had misjudged the willingness of his European trading partners to discourage the Americans from reacting to his intrusions into U.S. Territory.

This painting shows General Taylor on the white horse on September 23, 1846 observing his troops as they captured the key city of Monterrey. In subsequent days following a series of disagreements with President Polk, a large contingent of Taylor's troops were transferred to Gen. Scott. The following February despite a diminished force, Taylor won a brilliant victory over the Mexican army at the Battle of Buena Vista even though he was outnumbered by about four to one. All of this helped him become tremendously popular and elected President in 1848.

This painting depicts the landing of American forces under
General Winfield Scott at Vera Cruz on March 9, 1847.

And this famous painting shows a victorious General Winfield Scott
entering into Mexico City on September 14, 1847.

THE COMPROMISE OF 1850:

The Compromise of 1850 was a package of five separate bills passed by the United States Congress in September 1850, which served to mitigate a four-year confrontation between the slave states of the South and the free states of the North regarding the status of territories acquired during the Mexican-American War. The compromise, drafted by Whig Senator Henry Clay of Kentucky and brokered by him and Democrat Stephen Douglas, avoided/postponed secession and civil war and reduced regional confrontation for several years.

But the relief was short-lived. The slavery issue could not be fixed or compromised so easily because it was a question of morality. And so, the annexation of Texas served to produce a political crisis that eventually led to Civil War and a final resolution of the slavery question.

The Civil War and Texas: 1861-1865

As a Christian minister studying and writing about history, I have to say that I regret that my home state was once a slave state, and I regret that it split away from the U.S. for a while and joined the Confederacy over the subject of slavery. I also regret that it took another hundred years after the Civil War for African Americans in our state to acquire all their <u>God-given</u> rights and that it only came at all because of federal legislation. I wish these things had not happened and I wish the Civil War had not happened with all its death and suffering. I wish our history had been more perfect, more noble; but these things <u>did</u> happen and hopefully folks of this day in these present times can learn from those experiences of the past and reach for higher and greater things.

Learning from our mistakes isn't so easy though because humans have something built in that doesn't want to admit it when we've been mistaken. Indeed, *after* the Civil War was finally over, it became popular among Southerners including folks in Texas to say that the War hadn't really been about slavery but about "states' rights" as if it should have been a "right" for some states to have continued with slavery if they chose to. The "states' rights" rationalization goes on to this day; but <u>the actual documented truth</u> historically speaking is that *before* the Civil War everybody on both sides commonly and mutually and simultaneously agreed that the major focus of their confrontation was about the issue of slavery.

It's seems rather obvious, doesn't it? There was a major political battle that ensued in the U.S. Congress over this very issue when Texas was being considered for annexation into the Union and that confrontation <u>on a national level</u> continued right up to the Civil War, through the Civil War and after it was over. The whole country was officially designated as either "slave states" or "free states." We need to face this fact, learn from it and then talk about the issue of *states' rights* in some other context because slavery has <u>*always*</u> been an immoral institution in and of itself. It has little to do with the subject of *states' rights* because the "right" to own slaves has never been a valid moral position.

So as we've already seen Texas came into the Union as a slave state and caused a huge political confrontation all across the U.S. Being a slave state had happened because the largest segment of the new Anglo settler group streaming into Texas after 1821 had come from southern U.S. states and they brought with them an agricultural mindset that relied heavily on slavery. And of course, many brought their slaves with them.

Soon the position of slave ownership became the majority opinion in Texas even though only about 25% of the population actually owned any slaves. Coincidentally the group of settlers that either opposed slavery outright or the further expansion of it or leaving the Union in order to continue it was also about 25% of the population. Included in that opposition though was none other than Governor Sam Houston who had been elected in 1859, and only two years later we find him boldly refusing to endorse the Confederacy and Texas secession. Sam Houston was himself a slave owner who opposed abolition, but more than that he was a Unionist who wanted Texas to stay in the U.S. and avoid the war that was sure to follow secession. He was consequently thrown out of office by the State Legislature on March 16, 1861 after he refused to take an oath of loyalty to the Confederacy. Despite that he has remained a great hero in Texas even though he opposed the majority opinion in the state legislature, and all of his forecasts about the consequences of seceding proved to be accurate. He was a great visionary who possessed much wisdom with an uncanny ability to see how political choices would eventually turn out.

Despite the various negative aspects connected to the slavery issue though, I have no hesitation about celebrating the heroism and commitment of the people of Texas during those times even though the values of their collective effort don't match up with my opinion of how things should have been. People aren't perfect. They weren't perfect then and as hard as it is to believe, we aren't perfect now. To misjudge an issue of morality has happened before and it's still happening now despite this age of "perfected secular enlightenment" we're presently living through (written with tongue firmly planted in cheek). So I don't judge the people; that's Jesus's job and what I can celebrate is that the Texans of that day courageously defended what they believed was right with determination, heroism and honor.

Besides, it's easy for me now looking back to see the flawed values of that day and I often wonder how I might have believed had I grown up in Texas during Civil War times. I had Confederate military ancestors on both sides of my family including one notable lady who was a Confederate spy. The fact is, the culture and ways of thinking back then were a lot different than they are now. Even years later when I was growing up in Dallas during the last days of segregation in the 1940's and 50's I well remember that my values back then were strongly influenced by the political views of that day which said that it should be left to the states to embrace or disassociate from "separate but equal" segregation. I had to grow out of that way of thinking and eventually override the influences of the local culture and the politics and the older generations in my own family that so strongly favored segregation. That's why I'm careful not to judge the people of the Civil War days even though I DO judge what they believed.

As a final thought for this section, I want to make one last point. Slavery is an issue that the entire world has had to deal with at one time or another. It wasn't just a problem in the U.S. Only a few years before the American Civil War, most of Western Europe and the rest of the world were engaged in slavery. The truth is <u>there are STILL countries in the world today that are engaged in slavery all these years later</u>. In the U.S. it took a war in which more than 600,000 Americans lost their lives in order for slavery to be abolished. The loss of so many is hard to deal with, impossible to empathize. How could our ancestors have lived through such unimaginable hardship and tragedy and grief and loss and still have held the country together when the war ended? But the U.S. certainly DID survive and became the greatest country in the history of the world, a bastion of freedom and democratic republicanism.

Texas survived too, made a lot of adjustments and changes, and became the greatest state in the greatest country in the world. I am proud of my state for dealing with a problem of morality and eventually coming out on top with the right answer. I can also see clearly that God had a master plan for the U.S. and for Texas that not even the Civil War could derail.

Life in Civil War Texas

During the Civil War, Texas was sort of like the western breadbasket of the Confederacy, and supplied a lot of cotton, beef, leather, gunpowder and grain to the war effort. The Union blockade of the Texas Gulf Coast gave birth to adventurous blockade runners who slipped through the lines and ran Texas goods to foreign markets such as England and France. Later in the war, an extensive cotton trade with Mexico was set up by sending cotton overland into Mexico and then from one of the Mexican ports exporting it on to Western Europe thus circumventing the blockade.

Major wartime factories were set up in the Marshall-Tyler area of East Texas and many of the Confederacy's Trans-Mississippi Department's operations were run out of Marshall. Camp Ford, one of the largest prisoner-of-war camps in Texas, was also located near Tyler.

Unique to Texas, frontier defense was a key issue for many people. When federal troops left Texas at the beginning of the war, Indian attacks against the settlers increased. Some families moved to the nearest forts on a permanent basis, other communities provided frontier regiments like a local militia. Still, the Indians pushed back Texas development significantly during the war which had to be dealt with later on during Reconstruction. But, despite a lot of setbacks for the Confederacy, Texans had much to be proud of during the Civil War. The Union was never able to successfully invade and hold the Lone Star State. From the Red River to the coast, Texas repelled attack after attack. And economically, Texans came out much better than the rest of the South.

Also to consider is that much of the war effort in Texas revolved around women: women kept the ranches, farms and families going during those four years. Many *Tejanos* (Hispanic Texans of Mexican heritage) served in Confederate regiments, especially in South Texas. The Alabama-Coushatta Indians of East Texas also enlisted and served. African-American slaves did much of the labor that provided the food and goods for home and for export, as well as building Confederate fortifications.

A number of notable leaders were associated with Texas during the Civil War. John Bell Hood gained fame as the commander of the Texas Brigade in the Army of Northern Virginia and played a prominent role as an army commander late in the war. "Sul" Ross was a significant leader in a number of "Trans-Mississippi" Confederate armies. Felix Huston Robertson was the only native Texan Confederate general. Capt. T. J. Goree was one of Lt. General James Longstreet's most trusted aides. John H. Reagan was an influential member of Jefferson Davis's cabinet. Col. Santos Benavides from Laredo, Texas was a Confederate colonel and the highest-ranking *Tejano* soldier to serve in the Confederate military.

The office of Governor of Texas was in turmoil throughout the war with several men in power at various times. Sam Houston was replaced by Lieutenant Governor Edward Clark. Clark filled the rest of Sam Houston's term in 1861 and narrowly lost re-election by just 124 votes to Francis Lubbock. During his tenure, Lubbock supported Confederate conscription, working to draft all able-bodied men, including resident aliens, into the Confederate army. When Lubbock's term ended in 1863, he joined the military and was a successful officer. Ardent secessionist Pendleton Murrah replaced him in office. Even after Robert E. Lee surrendered in 1865, Murrah encouraged Texans to continue the revolution, and he and several supporters eventually fled to Mexico. Some really special friends of ours presently own the former home of the colorful Governor Murrah in Marshall, Texas and have their office there.

The beautiful home of the last Confederate Governor Pendleton Murrah (1863-65) is located at 1207 South Washington Avenue in Marshall Texas and is presently owned by our dear friends Larry and Rita Hooper where they operate *Eagle Management Company*.

Conditions were so tough during the last years of the Civil War that the cake served at Gov. Murrah's inaugural state dinner was made of corn meal.

Federal troops did not arrive in Texas to take control and restore order until June 19, 1865, when Union Maj. Gen. Gordon Granger and 2,000 Union soldiers arrived on Galveston Island to take possession of the state and enforce the new freedoms of former slaves. The Texas holiday *Juneteenth* commemorates this date. The Stars and Stripes were not raised over Austin until June 25.

President Andrew Johnson appointed Union General Andrew J. Hamilton, a prominent politician before the war, as the provisional governor on June 17. He granted amnesty to ex-confederates if they promised to support the Union in the future, appointing some to office. On March 30, 1870, the United States Congress permitted Texas' representatives to take their seat in Congress although Texas had not met all the formal requirements for readmission which required four additional arduous years to accomplish.

The two highest ranking Texans in the Confederate Army:

Gen. Albert Sidney Johnston

Lt. General John Bell Hood

Lt. Richard Dowling
Commander of the Victory at Sabine Pass

Francis Lubbock
Confederate Governor 1861-63

General Hiram Granbury:

Hiram Granbury organized a volunteer company for the Confederate Army and became its captain. He rose to the grade of Brigadier General and was one of the six Confederate generals killed at the Battle of Franklin on November 30, 1864.

My present hometown Granbury, Texas is named after the General even though he wasn't from here and he never visited. His name was just taken posthumously and in 1893 his remains were finally moved here.

Lawrence Sullivan "Sul" Ross

Gen. Felix Huston Robertson

Captain T. J. Goree

Postmaster General John H. Reagan

Col. Santos Benavides,
highest ranking Hispanic Confederate

Confederate Gov. Pendleton Murrah,
didn't want to stop fighting

President Andrew Johnson:

A Unionist Democrat from Tennessee succeeded to the presidency on April 15, 1865 after the assassination of Abraham Lincoln. He offered relatively <u>mild terms</u> for those states which had seceded to reenter the Union. However, he did not press further to guarantee the rights of African Americans and his <u>lenient policies</u> permitted the majority of Texans to assume their previous civil rights. Eventually though his lenient policies were replaced by more stringent requirements that produced resentment for generations.

General Gordon Granger:

Federal troops did not arrive in Texas to take control and restore order until June 19, 1865, when Union Maj. Gen. Gordon Granger and 2,000 Union soldiers arrived on Galveston Island to take possession of the state and enforce the new freedoms of former slaves. Six days later the Stars and Stripes flew once again over Austin.

Andrew Jackson Hamilton

On June 17, 1865 President Andrew Johnson appointed Andrew Jackson Hamilton, a former U.S. congressman from Texas and a Unionist who had fled to the North, as provisional governor of Texas. As a part of his ongoing plan to implement what historians call Presidential Reconstruction, Johnson instructed Hamilton to call a convention and undertake the necessary steps to form a new civil government in the state.

Reconstruction in Texas: 1865-1874

For the nine years following the Civil War, it can be said that Texas was a place in turmoil as the people worked to deal with the new political, social, and economic changes the war had generated. Many of those changes were for the good but they had to be faced and adjusted to suddenly. To start with, emancipation and the end of slavery forced a redefinition of the relationship between blacks and whites and changed the economic system relatively overnight. The related increase in labor costs along with the necessity of repaying the costs of the war weakened the economic, social and political status of the elite who had dominated life in the past and represented a power structure that had to be redesigned and replaced. In addition, the people had to pledge their loyalty to the U.S. and declare that secession from the union had been illegal, which at the time were disagreeable subjects most folks didn't want to have to face.

At the same time, life was even more difficult for the former slaves who had suddenly obtained their freedom but had no economic foundation to work from. For most of them, freedom from bondage provided limited opportunities for building new lives and they were not prepared for the economic adjustments that faced them in the short term. In sum, the coming Reconstruction Program presented the old order with some critical challenges and was not an easy time for anybody. Moreover, the victorious Unionists had no experience with nation rebuilding and often made matters worse in their enthusiasm to redesign everything overnight.

Anger at the war's outcome simmered in Reconstruction-era Texas. Before very long the freed slaves became the primary targets of widespread violence that followed the war's end. And, Texan voters did not help to ratify the Thirteenth Amendment (abolishment of slavery) or the Fourteenth Amendment (declaration of citizenship for African Americans). And despite the formal end of slavery in the United States, Texas along with other former Confederate states enacted restrictions for African Americans that severely limited their civil rights. Despite those tensions and after an uneasy five years, Texas was readmitted to the Union in March of 1870 even though they had not completed all the pre-established requirements.

Texas' return to the U.S. didn't end the turmoil though. Despite new railroad lines and industrial growth in the state, Texas remained a largely agrarian-based economy. Animosity toward the Republican Party and Reconstruction policies led to the election of a former Confederate officer as governor in 1874: Richard Coke. Slave labor was replaced with the sharecropping system, which kept African Americans in poverty and in subservience to white male landowners for years to come. Old conflicts with Native Americans that had not been tended to during the War years boiled over with new violence. A series of wars, known as the *Indian Wars*, pushed the remaining tribes in Texas off of their land and ended in death, imprisonment or surrender for a series of Native American leaders. Both the Apaches and Comanche's were expelled from the state.

Always fearful of a strong central government, Texans finally approved a new constitution in 1876, which severely limited the power of the governor. The Constitution of 1876 remains the basic law in Texas today. When the Presidential election of 1876 ended in Rutherford B. Hayes' victory, agreements between Democrats and Republicans resulted in the official end of Reconstruction. The period of Reconstruction was officially over in Texas, but restrictions and hardships for minorities would continue for almost a century even as economic expansion absorbed large numbers of immigrants from Europe and other parts of the U.S.

Finally the War was over and finally Reconstruction was completed. And more importantly a flawed system based on the enslavement of fellow human beings had been confronted and overcome. It took a while to change the established ways of thinking but change steadily occurred and today those ways of thinking and doing things are locked away in a compartment labeled "been there, done that and didn't like it." The people of Texas learned from it and as a part of the United States of America have prospered and grown and adjusted and accomplished and regained the direction God had set in motion from the beginning.

James W. Throckmorton

Throckmorton won the election of June 25, 1866 against Elisha M. Pease but his lenient attitude toward former Confederates and toward civil rights conflicted with the Reconstruction politics of the Radical Republicans in Congress. He angered the local military commander, Major General Charles Griffin, who persuaded his superior, Gen. Philip H. Sheridan, to remove Throckmorton from office and replace him with an appointed Republican and Unionist, Elisha M. Pease.

Elisha M. Pease

After the war, Pease became a leader in the state Republican Party and was appointed as the civilian governor of Texas in 1867 by General Philip H. Sheridan who was the military head of the Reconstruction government. Pease's policies as governor alienated both ex-Unionists and ex-Confederates and he resigned in 1869.

Edmund J. Davis

Davis was narrowly elected governor against Andrew Jackson Hamilton in 1869. He was a Unionist Democrat but as a Radical Republican during Reconstruction, his term in office was controversial. His opponents accused him of institutionalizing his political opponents, suppressing newspapers in violation of the First Amendment, and denying enfranchisement to regular Republicans. He was the last Republican Governor in Texas for more than 100 years.

Richard Coke

In 1866 Coke was elected associate justice to the Texas Supreme Court but the following year the military governor General Philip Sheridan fired him and four other judges as "an impediment to reconstruction." Now highly popular, he won the governorship in 1874 even as an ex-Confederate army Democrat and took office after a hotly contested post-election confrontation with his opponent. His administration balanced the budget and adopted a revised state constitution in 1876.

The Church in Texas: 1845 to 1874

Now that we've seen the political picture for this special part of Texas history, let's take a look at what the Church was doing all that time. Leading up to this period, it can be said that most Protestant preachers who had come into Texas with the early arrivals were sincere men of God who were called to provide ministry to spiritually hungry settlers. They came even prior to the Republic despite the fact that the Mexican law of the day prohibited non-Catholic ministry. But there were some who came, apparently in sufficient numbers to have been noticed by historians, whose lifestyles didn't match up all that well with their religious profession. The main problem was that in the beginning none of the Protestant denominations were well enough organized to provide credentials for all the newly arriving preachers.

So there were some charlatans and fakers among them who came and preyed on the strong desires of the settlers for spiritual rejuvenation. Those bad ones soon brought all ministers into some degree of disrespect, especially among politicians (if you can believe that), making it more difficult for the good ones to attract committed members into their congregations and to become respected leaders in their communities. All of this eventually led to legislative action to prohibit ministers from serving in political office. But despite the politicians' opinions of preachers, it's interesting that the Senate chamber in the Capitol when it was in Houston was the scene of almost weekly interdenominational preaching with both Protestants and Catholics sharing the pulpit. Time is a good healer and especially during and after the Civil War the vocation of minister-preacher grew in respect and prominence as the three main denominations (Methodist, Baptist and Presbyterian) became established and participants in the social fabric of the day.

The Christian Church here also had to deal with the slavery issue as new settlers came into the territory who were slave owners. As already noted, it's estimated that only about 25 percent of the total population of Texas were actual slave owners but the institution of slavery soon became a major force. Eventually the major denominations split over this issue and formed splinter groups that sided with the majority pro-slavery group. There were of course courageous ministers on both sides of this issue during the entire decade leading up to the Civil War who loved God and were seeking His Kingdom as they spoke out passionately convinced that their particular positions for or against slavery were correct and scriptural. But the Church was weakened by the splits and it took decades to repair the damage. Indeed, remnants of those splits remain even into current times.

In my view, the Church in the South missed God on this subject by a wide margin by trying to use the Bible to support slavery when they should have been preaching and teaching against it as well as against rebellion and against racial division in general. The Bible just doesn't teach the things the South wanted it to say. And so to be blunt about it, whether from secular pressure or cultural tradition, the theology that supported slavery and racial differences was contrived and plainly NOT scriptural. At a time when the Church should have been standing strongly against slavery to provide a positive influence for Believers in Texas and across the South, it instead invented a theology that supported an unbiblical point of view and made things worse.

For example, many churches held that the conduct of owning slaves and treating them well was a bible-based responsibility and that <u>being opposed to slave holding constituted heresy</u>. The basic idea behind their theology was that since there are no specific scriptures in the New Testament that prohibit slavery, and since slavery was a common practice when the Bible was written, then slavery was by default okay and even desirable. But to draw such a serious conclusion because something is NOT specifically mentioned in the Bible is pretty much contrived theology.

It should have been clear: Jesus was and is all about *agape* LOVE which is an unconditional, self-sacrificing type of love that Jesus exhibited for the Church and for the people He came to save, which is everybody on the earth including slaves (and Native Americans). It should have been obvious that the Africans who had been taken against their will from their homelands, brought to a strange land against their will, had their families split up against their will and sold in public for profit against their will were NOT grateful for that experience. In fact, many of them died on the way over to North America because of their harsh treatment at the hands of slave traders. It was never something they had wanted to do. The fact is they did NOT want to be slaves and they did NOT want to have to go through their slavery. And it was never out of LOVE that southern slave owners promoted their human commerce anyway. It was all about profit and business and economics and was therefore *obviously* unscriptural. Jesus came to set us all free, to deliver us from bondage, not to set up a new system where some of us would be able to enslave others in the name of Christianity.

The Church of Jesus Christ in the South had a golden opportunity to take a stand against slavery but chose the easy way of supporting it, both Protestants and Catholics. And by the way, Mexico was officially anti-slavery during and even before the Civil War as was the Mexican Catholic Church. And most of Europe had become anti-slavery too as had the Church there basing what they had come to believe on a revised theology that the South was calling heresy.

The historic facts are that as the South moved toward the end of the Civil War and Southerners began to try to account for the mounting number of losses in the field, according to their own writings they questioned whether God was judging them for not taking good enough care of all their slaves and for not respecting the institution of marriage among them as Scripture required. And they began to question why God had drawn them into the Civil War only to lose it despite their position of righteousness as they saw slavery to be. Well, let this be known: the Civil War was not God's idea. It was regular people who came up with it and all the while God was saying through His Word that the Southern Church was on the wrong track. Enslaving people is sin because it violates the Law of Love and sin brings about its own destruction without any help or judgment from God. The fact is more than 600,000 people were killed during the Civil War and none of that came from God.

Now I know that a lot of people will disagree with me on some of these points but the facts of history are what they are, and I've had to undergo a radical change in my own thinking to grow out of what I was taught as a young boy growing up in Texas. But my argument is mainly with their flawed theology. Study it out objectively for yourself and see what conclusions you come to because there are definitely two strong points of view on this subject and I don't represent to have all the answers on any topic, this one included. The point is: don't just rely on tradition and other people's opinions on this subject; study it out for yourself by reading commentaries on both sides of the issue and then determining for yourself which side is the truth and which isn't.

The Church isn't perfect; it never has been and it won't be until Jesus returns to take over its control. We do need to face the facts though to learn from them and there were both good and bad things that the Church did during the Civil War. Yes, the handling of the slavery issue was bad; but there were a lot of things the Church did well during this period and certainly the families of the hundreds of thousands of dead and wounded soldiers needed the comfort and direction that only their local churches and ministers were able to provide, and after the War ended they handled that responsibility very well.

Also, there were two particular areas that according to historians the Christian Church in Texas excelled in and the first had to do with education. The Texas revolutionaries had complained mightily about the failure of the Mexican government to provide education facilities. But after independence the new government of the Republic wasn't able to do any better because of a lack of money so the early responsibility for education had to be picked up by private and religious groups.

Fortunately the mainline church denominations were interested in both training ministers and providing a general education. Historians have calculated that there were nineteen educational institutions including Baylor University and an early version of Southwestern University that were started during the years of the Republic. And, between annexation in 1845 and the Civil War, an additional 117 institutions were chartered including seven universities, 30 colleges, 40 academies, 27 institutes, three high schools, two seminaries, an orphan asylum and a medical college. The leaders in the numbers of institutions organized were the Methodists, Baptists, Presbyterians, Roman Catholics, Lutherans and Episcopalians.

The other area the Church did particularly well on was providing solutions to the need for timely newspapers. Poor roads and mail service within the new State made communications extremely difficult and created a demand for news that the Church took the lead in addressing. The first denominational newspaper was the *Texas Christian Advocate and Brenham Advertiser* which was published by the Methodists in 1847. Although the publication had several name changes over the years, it was the forerunner of today's *United Methodist Reporter*. Earlier in 1841 Texas Baptists were allocated space in the *Baptist Banner and Western Pioneer* in Louisville, Kentucky and, in 1847 in the *Southwestern Baptist of New Orleans*. In January 1855 the *Texas Baptist* published its first edition and circulation rose to 2,600 before a shortage of newsprint during the Civil War forced suspension of its publication. The Catholic press in Texas started later in the 1890s with the *Southern Messenger* in San Antonio and the *Texas Catholic* in Dallas.

Now we've already looked at the general population growth over the period and despite the problems here and there, church growth was even more dramatic. The U.S. Census of 1850 reported 328 churches in the state with an aggregate capacity of 60,000 persons. By denomination the church numbers broke down like this: 173 were Methodist; 70 were Baptist; 47 were Presbyterian; and 13 were Roman Catholic. There were also five Episcopal churches, five Christian churches and 15 belonging to smaller independent groups.

By the 1860 U.S. Census there were 410 Methodist churches, 280 Baptist, 72 Presbyterian, 52 Cumberland Presbyterian plus a bunch of others for a total of 1034 churches across the state. Despite all this activity and growth though, organized Christianity did not reach some parts of Texas until after the Civil War because of distances and harsh conditions. But once established, churches carried out their traditional roles as civilizing influences, leaders of morality, and as major supporters and organizers of education.

In sum, the period of 1845 to 1874, a mere twenty-nine years, was a time of great change for both the State of Texas and the Church of Texas. The first sixteen years were under statehood as a part of the U.S., the last thirteen in estrangement from the U.S. with a broken relationship, a relationship that had been needed for protection from Mexico. Even so, the Church of Jesus Christ, both the Protestant and Catholic parts of it, more than survived and were able to influence the lives of Texans in a positive way despite the difficult political issues that had to be faced and adjusted to. In the end the Church emerged from the tumult of those years and provided the leadership that people needed in order to throw down strong roots, raise up wonderful families and build something special.

Texas today is recognized as one of the states with the highest and most committed church memberships in the entire U.S. It's more heavily Protestant in the north and east and Catholic in the south and southwest. The main Protestant groups in the 2010 Census were the Southern Baptist Convention with 3.7 million members plus 0.8 million of other kinds of Baptists, the United Methodist Church with 1.3 million members, the combined independent-non-denominational group with 1.5 million members, Pentecostals 0.7 million, Church of Christ 0.4 million plus about 2.0 million among all the other non-Catholic groups resulting in a total Protestant presence in Texas of about 10.4 million people. In addition, the Catholic Church which has fully recovered from those early settler days has a membership in the 2010 Census of 4.6 million. Put it all together and the Body of Christ in Texas today totals at least 15.0 million out of a total population of some 25 million people in the State. And in case you haven't thought about it too much, the Church is the reason we are today a people with strong traditional and family values particularly in the rural areas.

The State of Texas where settlers didn't want to go until the Mexican land grants gave them an offer they couldn't refuse is now the second most populous state in the Union. People are moving in now by the thousands upon thousands because we're seen as a land of opportunity where families can flourish and Christian values are still important. Scripturally speaking success is a blessing from God, and Texas is successful today because we still honor Him even in the face of determined secular moves against the values that have made us strong. The strength of Texas today is grounded in the communities and small towns, the places where people can still worship openly and pray publically and be involved in community things. God's hand has been upon this place always but in particular since 1494 when Columbus discovered Jamaica and set in motion a move of millions of Europeans and later from around the world to establish a New World where Christianity could flourish and be free.

Texans are proud people but proud in a good way: proud of our history and proud for what we have accomplished, proud of our people, proud of our families, and proud of our church heritage, proud of our folks who have served in the military, proud of our tough reputation, proud of the people who have faced hardship and overcome, proud of our diversity, proud of our work ethic and proud to be Texans. Once you've lived here there's a part of you that's been changed permanently and if you have to move away for some reason you'll take the change with you. *"You can take the boy out of Texas, but you'll never take Texas out of the boy."*

After being admitted to the Union the Body of Christ in Texas had to deal with the slavery issue. The fact is, Texas was turned down on its first petition for statehood by the U.S. Congress because it was a slave territory. The Church was split on this issue and went through a difficult time.

But there were two particular areas that according to historians the Church excelled in compensating for the slavery division somewhat by providing something positive in the face of profound adversity.

The <u>first</u> was the area of education and here are a couple of examples:

Martin Ruter

Robert Alexander

Francis A. Mood

Southwestern University located in Georgetown, Texas traces its roots back to the State Charter granted to Rutersville College in 1840 making it the oldest university in Texas. The school is affiliated with the United Methodist Church although the curriculum is nonsectarian.

Judge R. E. B. Baylor
(Namesake, Baylor University)

Rev. James Huckins
First full time Fund Raiser

Henry L. Graves
First President at Baylor

The charter for Baylor University was requested from the State of Texas in 1845 by Baptist leaders Rev. William M. Tryon (not pictured) and Judge R.E.B. Baylor who became the university's namesake. The Rev. James Huckins is considered the third founding father because he was the main fund raiser and his first major donor was war hero Sam Houston who gave a $5,000 donation to fund the start up.

The <u>second</u> area that the Church excelled in during the period was the start up, publishing and distribution of newspapers across the state. And following are a couple of examples:

Louis Blaylock

Copy of The Texas Christian Advocate
Published December 12, 1864

While living in Brenham, Methodist Minister Robert B. Wells (not pictured) began publishing the *Texas Christian Advocate and Brenham Advertiser* in 1847. It was the first religious publication in the state and combined aspects of a church newspaper with a secular weekly publication.

After several different name and ownership changes, it was moved to Galveston in 1854 and renamed *Texas Christian Advocate*. When Galveston was blockaded during the Civil War, the paper was forced to suspend publication and move its equipment to Houston. It did not resume publication until December 1864.

In 1866 the newspaper returned to Galveston, and a young man named Louis Blaylock began working for the printers. Blaylock went on to become a respected Methodist churchman and publisher of the paper. Under his leadership the paper's circulation expanded and its influence against saloons and gambling was notable. Eventually it became known as the *United Methodist Reporter*.

George Washington Baines pictured on the left came to Texas in 1850. He organized the first Baptist church in Marshall and was <u>editor of the state's first Baptist newspaper in 1855 called the *Texas Baptist*</u>. His grandfather (George Baines) came from Ireland. George W. Baines' mother was Mary McCoy. In 1861 George Washington Baines was President of Baylor University. His son Joseph Wilson Baines was the Secretary of State of Texas from 1883 to 1887. He was the father of Rebekah Baines who married Samuel E. Johnson and their son was Lyndon Baines Johnson, the 36th President of the United States.

POST CIVIL WAR TRAVELING PAPERS

Most church groups split over the subjects of slavery and the Civil War into north and south factions and some of those divisions continue to this day. The split in the Methodist Episcopal Church is reflected in the *Traveling Papers* shown below that were carried by a couple of my ancestors from the Tennessee-Mississippi area out to Texas in 1887. There was an M.E. Church South and an M.E. Church North and *Traveling Papers* conveyed one's membership in a particular faction that would be recognized at the destination. The fingerprint over the first line below may be 127 years old when this book is published.

This is to certify that
Hamp McGill, has been
an acceptable member of the
M E. Church South – Corinth
Circuit, Corinth Dist, North
Miss Conference.
May – 1887.
W. M. Young, P. C.

This is to certify that
W. L. McGill, has been an
acceptable member of The
M. E. Church South at
Boxes Chapel, Corinth Circuit
Corinth Dist, North Miss
Conference, – May – 1887.
W. M. Young P. C.

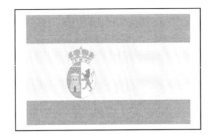

Spain had two flags during the periods 1519-1684 and 1690-1821

France 1685-1690

Mexico 1821-1836

Republic of Texas 1836-1845

Confederacy 1861-1865

United States 1845-1861 and 1865-Present

During all of this exciting history there have been six primary flags that have flown over the territory of Texas and Christianity was right in the middle of the entire process. Each group of people these flags represent had a profound impact on what has become one of the great success stories in the development of the United States.

Success was not always easy and the Conquistadores and Franciscans and Settlers and Pioneers and Cowboys and Ranchers and Farmers and Shop Keepers and Ministers of the past had to overcome significant personal discomfort to achieve their goals and help shape the destiny of Texas. To have left out any of these six flags would have made a big difference in the history we are so proud of today that has finally produced what those early visionaries could only have dreamed about.

Yes, there were hardships and there were mistakes. History is never perfect and neither is the Body of Christ. But without trials and mistakes the learning process would be a lot slower and there would have been no victories to enjoy. Victory requires that there first be a battle and people have been battling here now for almost 500 years. Native Americans have been battling here for millennia.

The result is a unique culture that is still striving for accomplishment and excellence and achievement perhaps like no other place. Everything we enjoy today has been worked for. Blood and tears and sweat have been shed. Christ will be glorified and a bright light is now shining on this place.

Part Eight:
The Cattlemen

Before we can conclude this project, there's one remaining group of special folks from early Texas history we need to talk about because of their particular influence on what we've eventually turned out to be. Historically there's no question that Texas has been closely connected to the cattle industry for a long time. In fact, when people from all around the world think of Texas now days, the context is probably going to be some combination of cattle and ranchers and cowboys and cattle drives and longhorns and stampedes and rodeos and roping and ten-gallon hats and cow ponies and all the rest of this special, almost mythical aspect of western culture that makes Texas such a unique place. Texas and cattle just seem to naturally go together.

On the other hand, it's really hard to find documentation to connect all that cattle history to any particular influence from Christianity. The basic reason is that the missions and churches of the day were established in the various organized communities that developed around the state but most of the people who worked in the cattle industry were typically located many miles away on remote ranches or involved in cattle drives often lasting several months on the trail and away from home. Church-going among the cattlemen was a sometimes event when Believers among them made special trips to be in town or at the nearest fort or settlement for Sunday morning services. Many circuit riders eventually came into Texas but they also tended to go to the settlements instead of out to all the ranches. In short, individual Christian growth was relatively more tied to one's personal commitment to prayer and Bible study and less to church attendance.

So on the surface it might seem that this particular group of folks was not influenced too much by the Christianity of the day. And yet the Cattlemen were largely thought of as being tough, principled people who told the truth, defended the women folk, stuck by their families and generally demonstrated many other Christian values. Eventually the great majority of these people and their succeeding generations after them wound up being a part of one of the strongest bastions of Christianity in the entire United States. Texas sits today at the western edge of the Bible-Belt and hosts some of the largest and most influential Christian ministries in the world, ministries that reach billions of people around the globe on a daily basis. So, it would be a mistake to conclude that because of inaccessibility to churches in those early days, there was no Christian presence in the remote ranching areas.

Keep in mind too that the *Second Great Awakening* didn't come to an end until about 1840. The early Anglo settlers responding to the Mexican land-grant program of 1821 were coming out of that environment to find a new future in the Texas territory. Many of them had strong Christian roots when they arrived. So this would be a good place to state a basic Christian principle: once a person is truly born again, they may commit a sin or two once in a while, they may even backslide from time-to-time; but they will almost NEVER give up on their faith. And that faith is strong enough to carry them through the wilderness times when there are no churches and a scarcity of other Christians to fellowship with. That's why throughout history God has ALWAYS had His remnant of true Believers to carry the Cross of Christ when things got sparse. And those early settlers were somehow able to get through those years of spiritual wilderness, when things were just getting started around here, to emerge on the other side and raise up succeeding generations of strong, tough-minded, no-nonsense Christian Believers who built this state and among other things raised up an incomparable cattle industry.

Now there were, and still are, two basic groups of *Cattlemen* that did all that: the ones who owned the ranches and the ones who worked for the ranches. The owners were the *ranchers* and the other group publicity-wise was epitomized by the *cowboys*. Those two groups of special *"cattle-folks"* have had a huge impact on the history of our state and even today Texas produces more cattle than any other state in the country by a pretty wide margin. We still have some big ranches and the Texas Cowboy is a featured institution in our modern culture. And it shouldn't be surprising that the Texas Longhorn eventually became one of our official "state mammals" (along with the *Nine-banded Armadillo* and the *Mexican Free-tailed Bat,* just so you know the whole story).

But what people sometimes lose sight of is that the rancher-cowboy way of life as it's depicted in all those beloved western movies of ours was the part of this story that developed largely *after* the Civil War. Before that there was a whole other ranching history that established a rock-solid foundation for the famous era that came later.

The Early Days

That word "ranch" is pretty common around Texas and most Texans know that a "ranch" is a place where livestock is produced as compared to a "farm" where crops are planted and then harvested a few months later. But did you know that the English word *ranch* is derived from the Spanish word *rancho?* They have slightly different meanings but they're closely related which you would expect since they sound the same. The word *rancho* to the Spanish-speaker is the headquarters, usually the home of the *ranchero* who owns the place where the livestock is produced while the English word *ranch* represents the entire area or the range that's owned or controlled by a *rancher* where livestock is produced. You would be correct in concluding from the influence of the Spanish language on this subject that ranching in Texas goes back a long way. First came the Spanish followed by the English...*centuries* later! First came the *rancho* followed by the *ranch*...centuries later!

The fact is cattle first came to Texas through Spaniards who began establishing their early *ranchos* down in what is now Mexico and driving herds up from there in the early 1540's.

Remember that *Cortes* the great Conquistador had defeated the Aztec Nation in 1520 so it didn't take long for the local production of Spanish cattle (and horses) to be initiated. In a little more than 20 years the first cattle drives from Mexico came up into the Texas territory at about the same time that those other famous Conquistadores like *Coronado* started showing up looking for gold. Those cattle provided food to the small Spanish settlements that were beginning to spring up around the state.

In 1682 the first of the Texas missions were constructed creating additional demand for cattle to be driven up from Mexico. So, as years went by a lot of cattle were driven up and released along the San Antonio River to be used as needed to feed the mission folks and the soldiers and the civilians in the main population areas of San Antonio and Goliad. And those cattle began to multiply all over South Texas until some smart *rancheros* got the bright idea along about 1730 or so to put some herds together from the surplus and drive them over to market in New Orleans where they were worth a lot more money. And with that, cattle had become a revenue-generating export commodity and the Texas cattle industry was officially born.

Before very much longer, ranching shifted from the *ranchos* down in Mexico to some new *ranchos* up here in Texas. In fact, the Spanish government made it possible for those new *ranchos* to get started and to flourish up here by making large land grants to a few wealthy Spaniards on the condition that they would use the land to produce livestock including cattle, horses, sheep and pigs. In a short time those new *ranchos* in Texas were a thriving industry that was soon attracting workers to come up from Mexico. Those original Texas *ranchos* <u>each</u> controlled Spanish land grants in the hundreds of thousands of acres and they provided both work and protection to the Spanish-speaking settlers who wanted to relocate. Most people don't realize that those first *ranchos* in Texas pre-dated the American Revolution and became the strong foundation for the famous ranching culture that eventually developed here.

Back in those early days Spain for some reason didn't want to let the Texas-based *rancheros* export very much of their cattle out of the territory. But in 1763 Spain officially took over the rule of the Louisiana Territory from France after the *Seven Years' War* (also known as the *French and Indian War*) and saw that as a good time to let down their trade barriers and allow the *rancheros* to send their cattle herds over to some new markets in the east. That worked really well for a while but before too long, Native Americans in South Texas increased their raids and agitation and forced many of the *rancheros* to leave their herds back at the *rancho* and head for protection at the forts and settlements. Finally, when Mexico took over the Texas territory from Spain in 1821 conditions began to improve so that so that cattle industry could get back to their business. And they had a lot more cattle to work with because during all the time the Indians had been agitating, the cattle had been multiplying...*into the millions*.

And as you already know the Anglo settlers finally started coming into Texas after the Mexican land grant program had started and that flow of settlers rapidly intensified as we came into the

1830's. Most of those settlers came out here to be farmers, American colonists who had been farmers before but had fallen on hard times in the aftermath of the War of 1812. But when they arrived in Texas and saw firsthand the potential for getting involved in the cattle industry, many of those experienced farmers decided to become ranchers and cowboys and that's when things started to change.

In the 1840's and 1850's the ranching industry began to expand on its exports to other states and territories. Remember that Texas became a state in 1845 which changed its relationship to potential markets in the U.S. The cattle drives to New Orleans and to the east beyond continued and through New Orleans over to the West Indies in the Caribbean Islands. A few brave ranchers drove herds in other directions through and around hostile Indian territories, some along the Shawnee Trail to feed lots in Missouri, Illinois and Iowa and from there on to markets in Philadelphia and New York. Another trail lay to the west all the way to the California gold strikes that started in 1849 and it went almost to the far Pacific Coast.

By 1860 the Texas Cattle Industry was about to become something special. But of course the Civil War was on the immediate horizon. In the years leading up to the War, the center of the Industry, the place where the money was, shifted from South and Southeast Texas to the north central frontier just west of Fort Worth in what is now Palo Pinto, Erath and Comanche counties. But all that cattle herding and cattle trailing to the east, the north and the west leading up to the Civil War hadn't made a dent in the Texas cattle population because those cows could multiply faster than they could be exported. That was why when the Civil War came along, Texas was the major supplier of beef to the Confederacy.

And so, the stage was set. The cattle industry had already had a profound impact on Texas and on our economic climate, and greater things were still to come after the Civil War. In fact, the Texas cowboy was about to become world famous. He was the one they wrote books about in the late nineteenth century and made thousands of movies about in the twentieth century. He was the one who got all the glory but none of it would have been possible if some earlier, less famous "cowboys" hadn't blazed the first trails and laid a foundation of hard work and sacrifice that made it possible for the Texas cattle industry to get started. We can enjoy the famous cowboys as long as we don't lose sight of the original "cowboys" who were a lot different than what came later in the movies.

The Early Cowboys

The first thing that was different about them was that they spoke Spanish. In fact the very first ones were actually Spaniards from Spain who had come over to the New World with the *conquistadores*. Before much longer though they were joined by *mestizos* which is the Spanish word for folks of mixed Spanish-Indian lineage. The Spanish had conquered the "Indians" all over Mexico and eventually even down into Central America, and soon they were starting families together and passing on their Spanish language and traditions to succeeding generations.

Another difference was that all those first "cowboys" were Roman Catholics. The Protestant Reformation had just gotten started over in Europe in 1517; so when the first trail drives came up from Mexico in the 1540's, it was still more than 75 years in the future before the first Protestants would make their way to the New World and another century or two after that before any significant number of them would start showing up in Texas. And also by the way, back then they weren't called "cowboys." They were called _vaqueros_ which is a Spanish word that means literally "_men who work with cows_" or "cow workers." You could also translate it as "cow men."

When the _vaqueros_ came to the New World, they brought with them a tradition of working with livestock that had begun in medieval Spain during the Moorish occupation. Hopefully you remember from a previous article that the end of that occupation freed up funds for Queen Isabella to use to pay for Christopher Columbus' first voyage. The fact is, there was a strong Arabic influence left behind in Spain from that occupation which filtered through the New World and Mexico to influence our culture here in Texas including the entire system of ranching that we became so well known for. Equipment that cowboys still use today including stirrups, saddles, spurs, and hackamores (from the Spanish _jaquima_) and a lot of other things can be traced to Arabic tradition with clear roots all the way back to ancient Persia. In a nutshell, the entire idea of herding livestock from horseback came from that tradition and was brought over to the New World and to Texas by the Spanish.

As we already know the Mexican land-grant program of 1821 began to attract Anglo-Protestant settlers to Texas. Before that the ranching and cattle herding of the day had been performed by those Spanish-speaking _mestizos_ that had emigrated up from Mexico. But a slowly increasing number of English-speaking traders and merchants from the U.S. had regularly traveled through the territory braving the elements and hostile Native Americans to engage in the trading of manufactured goods for the hides and tallow produced from the vast Mexican cattle _ranchos_. So the two cultures had already started to slowly get acquainted before 1821 and a few hardy English-speaking folks had even settled in the territory seeing that there was great potential here for a new life.

But in 1821 when the newly independent Mexican government affirmed the Spanish land grant program, the merging of the two cultures began to rapidly accelerate. New settlers began streaming in from the eastern U.S. and they brought with them their different language and their different form of Christianity. Most of them came with the idea of starting farms and planting crops like they had done before they came out west. But a number of those settlers quickly discovered that there was a potential fortune to be made by getting control of the large herds of wild horses and cattle they encountered scattered everywhere across the territory and they decided to go into ranching instead of farming.

Now think for a moment about all the things that happened next over a relatively short period of time that helped accelerate the merging of these two cultures:

- Only 15 years after the 1821 Mexican land grant program, Texas was already declaring independence from Mexico on March 2, 1836.

- For the next almost 10 years Texas was an independent republic dominated by English-speaking Protestant leaders, separated administratively from Mexico but not culturally. A new culture was already emerging though that was no longer Mexican but it wasn't traditional American either.

- Then in 1845 Texas was annexed by the U.S. and became a state involved in a new set of concerns and politics.

- And a year later in 1846 the Mexican-American War came along. When that ended two years later, the dominance of the *rancho* culture that had come up from Mexico over the previous three centuries pretty much gave way to a unique, newly-merged bilingual-American-Mexican-Protestant-Catholic culture that had just emerged. <u>Almost all of that change had happened in only 27 years</u>!

I bring up this brief history here to help us appreciate how quickly the *vaquero* culture was overtaken by a new uniquely Texan *cowboy* culture. Spanish land grants were replaced by American land grants, the previously dominant Spanish language was replaced by English, Catholicism was replaced by Protestantism as the majority form of Christianity, the *hacendados* and *rancheros* were replaced by Anglo-rancher-settlers, and the *ranchos* by ranches. Suddenly out of the three hundred year old *vaquero*-centered culture emerged a revamped cattle industry featuring the English-speaking, Anglo Texas <u>*cowboy*</u>. It was built on the foundation of the Spanish *vaquero* but it had a new look and definitely a new "swagger." The time of the American-centered *cowboy* culture had arrived in Texas.

If you want to try to pinpoint the time when the old traditional culture actually gave way to the new, you could make the argument that it happened during the Mexican-American War from 1846 to 1848 because that's when Mexico finally backed away from its territorial claims and began to recognize the U.S. annexation of the entire Spanish territory from Texas to California. What had been Mexican became American with a unique new culture and way of doing things. And after the end of the war, the cattle drives to markets outside the state became serious business for a redesigned Texas cattle industry.

But those drives didn't last too long because things soon started to change again, and change in a big way. In 1861 the Civil War started and the Texas cattle industry tried to concentrate on getting their cattle to markets in the Confederate states to feed the troops. There were plenty of wild cattle to round up for that purpose, some historians have estimated between two and four million head. But getting supplies to the troops was a particular challenge because Union troops blocked most of the cattle trails at different times and made it hard to get through. The result was that during the war the market for Texas cattle pretty much disappeared, prices dropped through the floor and the cattle herds continued to multiply way faster than they could be exported. By 1865 when the war ended there was a record number of cattle waiting out on the open range for some Texas *cowboys* to come out and catch them again. And by that time there could have been as many as six million of those "ornery critters" waiting out there for the war to end. As soon as it did end, the great cattle drives began again and this time they became the inspiration for all the books and movies that came later.

The Cattle Drives

Those drives began again promptly in 1865 and fortunately for the Texas cattlemen, the end of the Civil War somehow brought on a major change in the manner of U.S. meat-consumption. According to historians the national preference for pork was suddenly replaced by beef. So, cattle that had been worth four dollars a head or less in Texas could soon fetch as much as 40 dollars in Missouri and Kansas and other points to the north which put those Texas cattlemen in a traveling mood. There was already a qualified and able bodied workforce of skilled horsemen available made up of de-commissioned horsemen from the Confederate cavalry, freed former slaves and Tex-Mex *vaqueros.* And they were definitely looking for work. So, all that was missing was some leadership and a relatively small amount of capital from a few of the key ranchers to get those wild longhorns moving out from the Texas range and on to the rejuvenated markets where all those new beef-hungry people were waiting. To get to those new markets required the prudent choice of routes where there would be a lot of grazing, a lot of water and as few hostile Indians as possible.

The earliest and perhaps the most famous of the post-war cattle trails was the *Chisholm Trail* and it soon became a major route. It was established in 1865 by Rancher Jesse Chisholm and ran 600 miles from San Antonio, Texas to the principal market in Abilene, Kansas. At some places the "trail" was as much as 50 miles wide. Rivers and Indian lands had to be crossed; but good grazing, ample water and relatively level terrain were a partial offset. Drives were relatively cost effective too: a drive along the Chisholm Trail with two thousand or more cattle required only a trail boss and a dozen cowhands. And of course at the end of the trail the higher prices were waiting which made all the cowboys a happy bunch that was eager to get back home to Texas to get involved with the next drive.

Other trails to the north were developed to connect the Texas cattle industry at various starting points to a number of additional new markets. About the time the Chisholm Trail was getting started, the *Shawnee Trail* to Missouri was regenerating itself. It had been an important route for the earlier smaller-scale cattle drives before the Civil War. After the War, it became one of the major trails. In 1867 the *Goodnight-Loving Trail* opened markets for Texas cattle in New Mexico, Colorado and all the way up to Cheyenne, Wyoming. And in 1874 the *Western Trail* (aka Dodge City Trail) was forged by cattle-drover John T. Lytle to reach markets in Nebraska. By 1879 it had replaced the old Chisholm Trail in popularity because it had fewer farmers along the way for the cattlemen to have to deal with and in doing that it became the principal trail for Texas cattle on their way to those northern markets.

Millions of cattle were moved from north to south along those four major trails between the end of the Civil War in 1865 and the 1890's. The booming demand for beef drew many more settlers to Texas and cattle ranching became big business here attracting capital investment from back east and all over the country. Local economies of towns along the frequently used routes benefited substantially. And experienced cowhands were in big demand. As Texas approached the end of Reconstruction in 1874, it must have seemed like nothing could stop those famous, romantic cattle drives along those famous, romantic cattle trails. Not even cow disease in various forms over the years had stopped those drives. But then something happened just about that time that changed the industry and eventually brought about an end to the Drives.

In 1874 as Texas Reconstruction was ending, a patent was awarded to an Illinois farmer by the name of Joseph Farwell Glidden for his invention of barbed wire. It was first introduced in Texas in 1875. It was particularly popular with farmers who wanted to mark off their lands and it was initially popular with the cattle folks so they could have a way to hold their cattle in confined areas after the round ups and the branding. But before long those new barbed wire fences were crossing the famous cattle trails and interrupting the flow of cattle to the north. For a while there was a lot of confusion and a lot of animosity. People in the north wanted their beef and people in Texas wanted to send it to them. To make a long story short, the railroad became the solution. The cattle wound up going to where they were needed but by a new and more efficient means of transportation. And those four principal cattle trails were eventually de-emphasized to make way for the future.

The cattle industry survived the closing of the cattle trails and the end of the cattle drives. In fact, it came back stronger than ever and became the economic bedrock of post-Civil War Texas. And the Texas Cowboy: he survived too and became ever more famous and romantic as the books and movies were written and produced by the thousands. The truth is the old forts and settlements and towns around the state benefited from the cattle industry, and cattle revenue was what made it possible for those places to grow and become places where families could throw down roots and grow and do something special. Texas had been a place of remote, scattered pockets of population, a place that settlers didn't even want to come to until the early 1800's. But cattle provided economic success and with that success the population centers became stronger. When that happens God's Church can come in to teach the Word, build local churches, encourage morals and ethical conduct and civil laws and reconciliation. The cattle industry played a significant role in creating a place of economic success where the Church could thrive and reach its current destiny as a center of worldwide Christian ministry.

It all goes back to first those cows that came over from Spain to Mexico and from Mexico to Texas almost five hundred years ago. God always has a plan and He's always working on it. Most of the time we can't figure out what He's doing, but He's doing it anyway. And then later on we can look back and see what He _was_ doing when we couldn't figure it out. Later on we can see His finger prints all over everything, His plan developing step by step. What would Texas be today had there been no cattle industry here? Fortunately we don't have to try to figure that out.

One of those famous Texas Longhorn

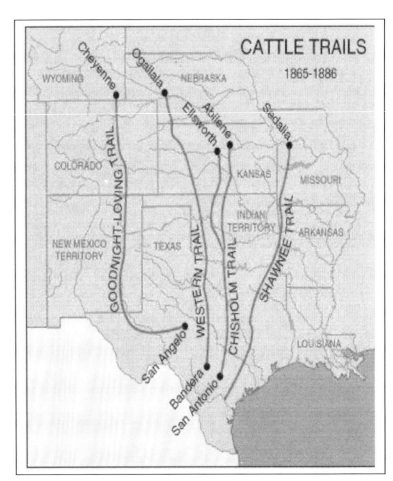

The major cattle trails out of Texas and up to markets in the north after the Civil War

Depictions of Mexican *vaqueros* above and on the left working and driving their cattle from horseback and traveling through town in the early Texas Territory

The famous Texas cowboy in action on a cattle drive

The cook and the chuck wagon were the center of power
on the Texas cattle drive second only to the Trail Boss

The King of the Trail

On the left, the introduction of barbed wire fences in 1875 was the beginning of the end of the free range and those famous cattle drives.

Audie Murphy

Gene Autry, the Singing Cowboy

Tex Ritter

Bob Wills

Dale Evans aka Mrs. Roy Rogers

President Lyndon B. Johnson, Rancher

Roger Staubach

Troy Aikman

Tony Dorsett

Emmitt Smith

Randy White

Larry Allen

Part Nine:
The Oilmen

As this article is being written in early 2015, Texas is widely reported to be one of the most economically *prosperous* states in the nation. It wasn't always that way and as already discussed in previous articles, it was difficult to convince early Anglo settlers to even come here. Not only were there hostile Indians to deal with but also there were vast distances involved and a country and capital city they weren't used to where the people spoke a different language and required the settlers to submit to Roman Catholicism. Things started to change in 1821 when Mexico won its independence from Spain, renewed the Spanish land grant program and coupled that with a direct invitation for Anglo farmers, ranchers and business people to come and settle in the Texas territory.

That's when the population finally started to grow attracting rugged individuals from the U.S. who had often experienced life's difficulties and were looking for new horizons and opportunities, especially financially. In short, they were seeking *prosperity* and one thing you may not know is that *prosperity* is a bible word that in one form or another is mentioned in Scripture almost one hundred times. In every instance God referred to it as a BLESSING. The fact is when God blesses people, it almost always involves financial increase and sometimes people get really, REALLY blessed. My point here is that the *Prosperity* of God has ALWAYS been a part of the destiny of Texas. Even today people are being attracted to Texas in great numbers because they believe their chances for experiencing increased financial *prosperity* are significantly greater here than wherever they're coming from.

A Tradition of Prosperity

It all started with the Spanish bringing all those Longhorn cattle up from Mexico to San Antonio back in the 16th century to feed people who were moving there and then later the folks who were coming to live in that growing chain of missions they started building all around the state. Eventually there were millions of those Longhorns out on the open range because they could multiply faster than they could be rounded up and brought to the end users in Texas and in a few nearby places including New Orleans where they could be exported to foreign markets. As we saw in the previous article, the cattle industry eventually became a big deal in Texas that helped fuel a vigorous economic expansion that continues to this day.

Those early days were followed by the Spanish and Mexican land grants of 1820–21 that made it possible for incoming farmers and ranchers to own and control large tracts of land at a relatively low cost where the large herds of cattle could be better monitored and controlled. A few years later after the Mexican-American War had ended in 1848 and with Texas as a state in the union instead of an independent republic, the cattle industry started to become something special and a foundation was built for a *prosperous* economy on a long-term basis. Unfortunately though that process was temporarily interrupted in 1861 by the Civil War. Even though Texas had enough livestock on hand to supply the entire Confederacy, the Union Army successfully blocked most of the attempted shipments to the various war fronts so those wild longhorns were pretty much left to themselves to continue multiplying. By the end of the War there were more than four million (some say up to six million) of those wild critters out on the range waiting for some cowboys to come by and take them to market.

And that's exactly what happened because it was immediately after the Civil War in 1865-66 that those great trail drives we discussed in the previous article started being put together. The objective was to get those Longhorns up to northern markets where the people had suddenly decided they wanted to eat more beef. In that way, the road to *prosperity* in Texas was quickly resumed despite Reconstruction. And in 1873-74 when those now famous cattle drives started winding down after the invention of barbed wire fences, the railroad came to the rescue with the capability of carrying even more cattle to the northern markets. Eventually the railroad itself became a significant industry here and a major agent of continuing *prosperity*.

Texas also became a major farming area after the Civil War as experienced Anglo settler-farmers streamed into the state in increasing numbers to purchase land at temporarily depressed values. Certainly, there was plenty of land to go around and on a significant part of that land were some of the great forests in the entire country that made it possible to raise up yet another *prosperous* industry: lumber manufacturing. Before too many decades had passed so much lumber had been sold that reforestation was required in East Texas which produced another generation of *prosperity* on into the twentieth century.

God had provided generously for *prosperity* in Texas. Of course over the years there were a few down times here and there but overall the second half of the nineteenth century was a time of great growth here featuring the establishment of what some folks now call a *prosperous* mindset: people who came here _believed_ they could *prosper* and be successful and so they did! As the Bible says: as a man thinks, so is he (Proverbs 23:7). If you sincerely expect something to happen and you can find in the Word where God can be behind it, then BY FAITH it will surely happen.

The Birth of a Special Industry

But there's more to this story still to be told! Certainly the cattle, railroad, farming and lumbering industries were important components in the development of *prosperity* in this state. Fortunes were made, families of substance and consequence were raised up, captains of industry were created and a class of *nouveau riche* (new money) began to emerge out of the confusion and tragedy of the Civil War. But as it turned out, the realization of God's *prosperity* in Texas was just getting started because the most *prosperous* thing that ever happened here was the discovery and exploitation of the natural resource we call "black gold" and the related development of an even more momentous industry that has made our state one of the foremost economic successes in history. To be sure, most of the *prosperity* from oil producing and refining came in the 20th century which is beyond the scope of this series of articles. But the beginnings of it, the first baby steps of this significant new industry that would change the world and industrialize Texas were taken long before that and they reveal that it was all part of the plan of God for establishing His Kingdom in the New World.

Remember that worldwide flood we discussed back in the first article? Noah and his wife and their three sons and their wives, a total of eight persons were the only people to survive that flood because God had ordered them well ahead of time to prepare for it by building a big boat. Nobody else was listening or believing because in the history of the world from the Garden up to the time of Noah, it had NEVER rained. But Noah's family did as they had been told and they brought with them on the boat some pairs of animals and plant life according to the Lord's instructions. All the rest of life on the earth at that time – humans, animals and plants – perished in the flood. Over their remains were quickly deposited layers of sediment and debris that were subjected to tremendous geologic pressure as the continents began to shift and separate as a result of the flood and related climate changes. And in the course of time, some of those organic remains became a virtually inexhaustible quantity of petroleum lying in pools below the surface of the ground all around the world.

Finally, almost four thousand years after the flood, the results of a process which according to Scripture God Himself had initiated were ready to be "discovered" in Texas by some of Noah's descendants who had been brought here from another part of the world to make the official discovery. Of course, secular folks want it to have been much longer for that process to have run its course, like hundreds of millions of years. But as I've mentioned before: I ALWAYS go with the Bible and it gives us the much shorter time-line we looked at back in the first article.

To continue with the story, you hopefully will also remember one of our old friends from the second article by the name of *Luis de Moscosso* who was the leading survivor of the *DeSoto Expedition*. He and his group managed to make their way overland from Florida through Mississippi and Louisiana and eventually to Texas, but they found it inhospitable over here for some reason and soon turned back to the Mississippi River so they could build some boats and return to Mexico City by a different route. In July of 1543 with only 322 survivors remaining from the 600 folks that had originally landed in Florida, they sailed along the coasts of Louisiana and Texas on their way back to Mexico. But their new handmade boats were leaking so they had to go ashore in the vicinity of Corpus Christi Bay off the Texas coastline where they observed a thick black sticky substance, with a consistency of something we know today as asphalt, floating in patches on the surface of the water. According to their description, what they had found was most likely crude oil that had been released naturally from cracks and fissures in the floor of the Gulf of Mexico which is a natural occurrence that still goes on to this day. To their credit, they quickly deduced that the black substance they had found could be used to caulk their vessels and stop the leaks. So the Moscosso group is credited with making the first recorded sightings of oil in Texas and they even used it to get back home to Mexico City. By doing that they called attention to an indigenous substance here that would eventually change everything!

To be accurate with this story, some of the local Indians already knew about the oil before *Moscosso* came on the scene and historians say they were using it for medicinal purposes at least as far back as 1410. But *Moscosso* has gotten the credit for the "discovery" and over the following centuries, settlers and visitors to Texas commonly came across seepages of crude oil all around the territory. So it was a pretty well- known fact that oil lay beneath the surface of the ground here. For a long time though it was seen more as a problem than a benefit because the presence of the oil hindered the digging of water wells that were needed for the exploding agricultural industries. Cattle DO prefer to drink water and so do crops and people. Eventually during the 1850's a process to distill kerosene from crude oil was invented by *Abraham Gesner*, a Canadian physician and geologist from Nova Scotia. A short time later, a worldwide demand for kerosene fueled lamps developed and the commercial potential of all that seeping crude oil in Texas suddenly began to be seriously considered.

The first commercial oil well in the U.S. was drilled in northwestern Pennsylvania in 1859 by Edwin Drake using a new process he had invented. It didn't take long for some Texas entrepreneurs to take notice of that development, and the first one to drill a producing well here was Lyne T. Barret in 1866 in Nacogdoches County. The following year, Amory Reily Starr and Peyton F. Edwards brought in a well at nearby Oil Springs, Texas. Other wells followed in that area making Nacogdoches County in East Texas the site of the first commercial oil field, the first pipeline and the first effort to refine crude oil in the state. Only two years had passed since the end of the Civil War and a difficult Reconstruction Program had been implemented, but the oil industry in Texas was gathering together its foundation in the very midst of the difficulty.

In the following decades during Reconstruction and re-admittance back into the Union, a number of wells were drilled but none of them including the original efforts in Nacogdoches County proved to be commercially viable on a long-term basis. Finally though, the first economically significant discovery came in 1894 in Navarro County near Corsicana. The Corsicana oilfield developed gradually and peaked in 1900 when it produced more than 839,000 barrels of oil. The first relatively modern refinery in Texas was opened there in 1898 and operated by the Joseph S. Cullinan Company. Cullinan helped found the *Texas Company* which eventually became *Texaco Oil & Gas*.

The success of the Corsicana field and the increasing worldwide demand for oil led to more exploration all around the state. But the oil discovery that jump-started Texas' transformation into a major petroleum producer and industrial power was the famous *Spindletop* oil field. Exploration in the area of the upper Gulf Coast near Beaumont had begun in 1892; and after drilling several dry holes, Louisiana mining engineer and oil prospector Capt. Anthony F. Lucas drilled the discovery well of the *Spindletop* field. Initially, the Lucas No. 1 well produced more than an estimated 75,000 barrels of oil per day. Peak annual production was 17.5 million barrels in 1902 and the Texas petroleum industry and all its related prosperity that was to come in the 20th century was on its way.

Acknowledging the Blessing of God

When oil came gushing out of the Texas ground early in the 20th century, the changes here were profound. Petroleum began to displace agriculture as the principal force that drove the state economy and the lives of Texans were even more affected than they had been by cattle and the railroads in the 19th century. The fact is Texas oil has benefited the lives of millions of Texans who were never directly involved in the oil business, Texans who never received either a paycheck or a royalty from the petroleum industry. In sum, oil has changed the culture of the state, and it continues to affect most Texans' lives today in ways that aren't necessarily obvious. Among other things, it has brought us a culture of *prosperity* that people here have become accustomed to, have benefited from and that others are attracted to.

Let there be no misunderstanding here: in my view the discovery of oil in Texas has been a tremendous BLESSING of God. It wasn't left here by accident or by a random geologic process. It was put here and in many other places around the world by the Lord Himself as a result of a process He Himself initiated with His great Flood. Oil is one of the three principal fossil fuels that abound on the earth with the others being natural gas and coal. They are joined by the lesser fossil fuels propane gas and hydrogen. All of them are blessings from God for such a time as this and all blessings have a purpose. The divine underlying purpose for fossil fuels is to help empower people to expand the Kingdom of God on the earth.

Now blessings from God are often seen as curses by the secular community and more often than they ought to be in the Christian community as well. Indeed, all three of the major fossil fuels are under attack today from secular environmentalists and from others who have been caught up in their rhetoric. The accusation is that the use of fossil fuels is harming the planet in a variety of ways including "global warming" and pollution and oil spills and the like. Certainly at first glance the petroleum industry in operation is not a pretty sight and it was particularly ugly in the early days until technology could catch up with the economic incentive for finding and extracting more oil. But blessings don't have to be "pretty" to be blessings. Petroleum is messy but it's still a huge benefit as the American Indian and *Luis de Moscosso* found out a long time ago. It is after all human beings that have to extract and transform and transport and use those fossil fuel blessings and people are going to be imperfect and make a mess of things until we eventually figure out how to use them the way they were intended.

So here we have God-given blessings that are widely seen as curses. But we DO have to have fuel to drive the economy. Can you imagine a planet without the availability of these fossil fuels? Were it not for them, we would all still be living back in the Stone Age as the Native Americans were when Europeans first came to the New World. So what is the alternative to fossil fuels? Invariably the attempted answer to this question is an array of *"alternative fuels"* that are mostly all manmade.

- How about the wind? Too many unsightly windmills and too expensive.
- How about ethanol? Disturbs the market value of a food commodity, too expensive.
- How about batteries? Inefficient and too expensive.
- How about water current? Requires a special infrastructure, too expensive.
- How about wood? Insufficient availability, a worse pollutant, too expensive.
- How about biodiesel? Disturbs the market value of food commodities, too expensive.
- How about atomic energy? Problem with disposing the waste material, too expensive.

Do you really think that human beings are capable of inventing an energy form that is more efficient, less expensive and more appropriate than Almighty God? Answer that question for yourself but I would expect Christians to see that if God is behind the fossil fuel option then it isn't going to kill the planet. Can we improve on the efficiency of how we extract and transform the raw materials? Yes of course we can and those improvements are ongoing including the coal option that is plentiful and just as much a part of God's plan for these times as crude oil and natural gas are. And yet our own government seeks to shut down the entire coal industry in the short term and the petroleum industry in the longer term based on the false assumption that they are harming the planet. Another question: do you really think that God would make a BLESSING available to us that would harm His own creation? That's not the way God operates. The flood was a special one-time circumstance that God promised to never repeat.

Isn't it fairly obvious though that the earth is deteriorating? Yes, it's obvious but it has NOTHING to do with the use of fossil fuels and it's time that Christians stopped agreeing with non-believers and started agreeing with their Bibles. The truth is, the earth is cursed by sin and has been progressively deteriorating since Adam and Eve disobeyed God in the Garden of Eden allowing sin to enter upon the earth (Romans 5:12). It's not ever going to get better and in fact the Bible says that the earth will eventually have to be replaced (Revelation 21:1). Yes, there will be a new earth someday because this one is irretrievable, irreparable and God will want to start over.

The bottom line is that the presence of fossil fuels is a BLESSING from God and we need to be thanking God for it instead of trying to figure out ways to set it aside and replace it. Let's stop worrying about the earth because God is not the one harming it and rather, focus on helping people understand how God operates. I am thankful beyond measure that God has called me to live in a state that has a *prosperous* mindset that fossil fuel has made possible and encouraged. The BLESSINGS in Texas abound and they make it a great place to call home!

Lyne T. Barret, founder of
Melrose Petroleum Oil Company
and Father of the Texas oil Industry

Lynn T. Barret home in Nacogdoches, Texas

Joseph S. Cullinan,
opened the Corsicana oil field
and helped found Texaco

Anthony F. Lucas
Initiated drilling on Spindletop Hill in 1899

Spindletop No. 1

Part Ten:
The Christians

When we started this series of articles together, I was making the point that the area we now know as Texas was squarely involved in a long-term Plan of God to build His Kingdom in the New World. If you can't see all these events we've discussed as part of an intelligently designed Master Plan than excuse me but maybe your spiritual wood is still a little wet. You need to open up those spiritual eyes and look a little closer at how all these things came together over a span of almost seven hundred years to get to where we are today. It was no accident; it was no coincidence.

It's great to live in Texas and be a part of what's going on here. We have a wonderful culture that's full of tradition and pride in our accomplishments. Most of our history has been good, inspiring us to push ahead for ever greater accomplishments. The part we wish we had not gone through we've learned from and hopefully we'll be wise enough not to go down those "rabbit trails" again. Our interest in history here is as great as any place I've ever lived and perhaps only Virginia where so much history has happened comes close to the interest and respect for history we have in Texas.

But the truth of it is the history we enjoy isn't really about us or about the people who preceded us in the unfolding of the story. We can celebrate it and remember the heroes and the cowboys and the desperados and all the rest of it. From the beginning though it was more about Jesus and about His Kingdom on the earth and about His Word than it was about all that other stuff we love to celebrate. And unless you're a real Christian you're not going to fully understand the point I want to make here in this last article.

Well over half the population of the state today (about sixty percent) professes to being involved in Christianity, either Protestant or Catholic or Independent. But there's a difference between being involved in Christianity and being a Christian. Christianity has done a lot of things over the centuries both good and bad. But according to the Bible, a Christian is someone who has accepted the forgiveness of sins that have already been paid for by Christ and has chosen to live life under the authority of His Word. A lot of people who claim to be Christians are Christians in name only and what's important is that each of us makes a decision at some point in life to either become true Christians or continue to live in darkness. It's by that decision that we receive salvation and eternal life, which is to say that folks can be involved in Christianity without ever becoming true Christians and without ever receiving salvation. That is what the Bible actually says and we either accept that or reject it.

Now a lot of people involved in Christianity believe that they will be saved because they've done a lot of good things in their lives. But that idea is also totally contrary to what the Bible actually says. There are no deeds we could possibly perform that are good enough to pay for the sins that we have each committed. It's impossible and that's why Jesus, a perfect man had to come to this earth and pay for our sins with His blood. Only His good deeds were good enough and only His blood was pure enough. Indeed, the Bible says that the only way to permanently pay for sin is by the shedding of somebody's perfect blood which turned out to be Jesus.

Here at the end of this little book, I wanted to provide to anyone who wants it an opportunity to receive God's total and complete forgiveness and become a true Christian. According to what your Bible actually says, all you have to do to be saved is agree by speaking it out that Jesus is your Lord and by believing in your heart that God raised Him from the dead (Romans 10:9). Just say the following *Sinner's Prayer* preferably out loud and believe it with all your heart:

Jesus I declare today with all my heart that I believe in you and that God raised you from the dead. I acknowledge that my sins have been forgiven and I ask you to come into my life today and be my Lord and Savior. Thank you for salvation and eternal life.

If you were sincere as you prayed this prayer, God has already come into your life and you are a new creation, a totally new person recreated in His image, a true Christian. Now ask the Lord to lead you to a good faith-based, bible-teaching church where you can be equipped to fulfill your potential in the Kingdom of God.

And, when you get a chance have someone help you look up the following scriptures because they confirm what you've done by saying this prayer today and believing what you said:

Romans 10:9
2 Corinthians 5:17
Ephesians 2:8

Now if you did say this prayer today, go and tell someone the good news. You will want to continue to celebrate the history of Texas. It's special and it's worth celebrating. God had His hand on it the whole time and that's one of the reasons it turned out so special. And now that you can see that God was involved, the history of Texas should be way more special to you than it ever was before.

Long live Texas! And thank you for reading these articles. We hope they blessed you as much to read them as they did me to write them. May God bless your every endeavor!

Study Questions and Answers

Study Questions for Part One

1. The main purpose of God has always been to _____.

2. According to the Bible, what is the age of the earth?

3. How many years ago did the worldwide flood occur?

4. How many people were saved from the worldwide flood by entering Noah's ark?

5. What period of time passed between the worldwide flood and the building of the Tower of Babel?

6. Approximately when did *The Scattering* occur?

7. When Columbus arrived in the New World in 1492, he found people on the islands and he called them _____.

8. What the name of the predominate group of Native Americans in the Caribbean islands that Columbus found?

9. The name *Texas* comes from a word in one of the Native American languages. What is that word and what does it mean?

10. What is the name of the Native American tribe from which the name for Texas was taken?

Discussion Questions for Part One

1. What was *The Scattering*, why did God do it and what specific actions did He take? You will want to consult your Bible to get the full answer.

2. How do you react when you hear the word "savages" used to describe Native Americans?

Answers to Study Questions for Part One

1. Establish His Kingdom on throughout the earth
2. About 6,000 years
3. About 4,500 years ago
4. Eight
5. Three hundred years

6. Between 2200 and 2100 BC
7. Indians
8. Taino
9. Taysha, friend
10. Caddo

Study Questions for Part Two

1. The first European to actually see Texas was _____ and he arrived here in the year _____.

2. That first European visitor was originally from the country of _____ and he was sent here by the governor of _____ whose name was_____ ___.

3. He was sent out to find _____ and to_____ _____.

4. That first European didn't accomplish either of the things he was sent to do but he did wind up _____ which opened the door to the future exploration of Texas.

5. The personal writings of Columbus over a long period of time prove he was a devout and well-informed _____.

6. According to his writings Columbus believed that he was called by God to _____ _____.

7. For six years Columbus tried repeatedly but unsuccessfully to convince King John II of ____ _____ to provide funds for his voyage to the New World. Finally though, he was able to convince Queen _____ and King _____ of Spain to provide his funding.

8. How can we connect the ministry and work of Columbus to the history of Texas? _____ _____

9. What did the Europeans bring with them that changed the course of history in the New World? _____

Discussion Question for Part Two

What reasons would you give for the fact that it took more than 1500 years after the resurrection of Christ for Christianity to reach the New World?

Answers to Study Questions for Part Two

1. Alonso Alvarez de Pineda, 1519
2. Spain, Jamaica, Francisco de Garay
3. A passageway to the Far East, a permanent colony in the new area he discovered
4. Drawing a map of the (Texas) Gulf Coast
5. Christian
6. Spread Christianity around the world
7. Portugal, Isabella, Ferdinand
8. Columbus discovered and established the colony of Jamaica from where the first European was sent 25 years later.
9. Their Christianity

Study Questions for Part Three

1. What was the name of the Spanish Explorer who conquered the Indian nation that had built their capital city on the site of what later became Mexico City? _____
    _____

2. What was the name of the Indian nation that was conquered when their king was killed by the explorer in Question number one? _____

3. In addition to building Mexico on top of the destroyed former Indian capital, there are two other important changes that the Spanish brought to that area. What were they?

4. Name the explorer that survived an eight-year, 6,000 mile trip and had to go overland to get back to Mexico City. _____

5. The unfortunate explorer _____ drowned at sea after antagonizing most of the Native Americans on the west coast of the state of _____.

6. The first European to see the Grand Canyon was the explorer _____during his quest for the _____.

7. When he didn't find any gold at the first location, the same conquistador in Number 6 went looking for it at a second place called _____.

8. There was one conquistador who came west from Florida, Georgia, Alabama, Mississippi and Arkansas and then ventured into Texas in 1542. His name was _____
    _____ and he had originally been under the command of _____who died in the midst of all that exploring and never made it to Texas.

9. Which conquistador found the most gold, how much did he find and where was it found?

10. The main contributions of the conquistadores is that they brought their _____ and their _____.

Discussion Questions for Part Three

1. What happened to all the gold? Do you think the Indians hid it, fed the explorers greed for gold with some non-existent myths to get them out of the area or played a joke on them? Or what?

2. Imagine and consider the hardships encountered by the conquistadores: there were no roads, no phones, no maps, no means of communication, hostile Indians, no forts of refuge, no knowledge of the area, no Spanish-speaking people to talk to outside their own groups, no sources of provisions, no transportation other than horses or by foot for thousands of miles, harsh weather, no shelter other than what they could pull together wherever they temporarily stopped before pushing on and there was no gold after years of looking for it. But there was a lot of death because their brethren kept dying and surely they dug graves for them or made some arrangements.

How would you have handled such an environment? What would make you consider this kind of life? Would a little gold have been enough?

But can you also see the unique and key role they played in the development of the New World? How could it have ever been developed without somebody going out to make those first explorations?

Answers to Study Questions for Part Three

1. Hernan Cortes
2. The Aztecs
3. Introductions of Christianity and the Spanish language
4. Cabeza de Vaca
5. Pánfilo de Narváez, Florida
6. Coronado, Seven Cities of Cibola
7. Quivara
8. Luis de Moscoso de Alvaredo, Hernando de Soto
9. None of them found any gold anywhere
10. Language, religion (Christianity)

Study Questions for Part Four

1. The Spanish colonization program was really slow to get going in the New World but finally in the year _____ under the leadership of _____, the first group of Franciscans went out to establish a colony but to the west of the Texas Territory.

2. Finally in the year _____ they established their first key colony which became _____ _____.

3. The first missionary attempts into Texas occurred in the year _____ and again in the year _____ and were led by _____.

4. The missionary group in the above Number 3 came from which mission colony and in response to a "request" from which tribal group that lived near which present day Texas city?

5. What was the driving force that led the Franciscans to Texas and made them want to establish missions here?

6. The name Texas is derived from the _____ languages and it means _____ _____. In the original languages the words translated now as Texas were used as a greeting to convey something like, "_____."

7. The most famous of all the Spanish missions is the Alamo where over one hundred Texas heroes were killed in the famous battle with the Mexican army in 1836. What was the original Spanish name for this famous mission and in what year was it constructed?

8. In what year were the first two Spanish missions established in the Texas territory?

9. What was the name of the French colony established on the Gulf coast of Texas, what was the name of the famous French explorer who originally led the colonization group and in what year was it established?

10. There were four objectives for the development of Native Americans that the Franciscans tried to accomplish by the operation of their missions. What were they?

Discussion Questions for Part Four

1. How would you assess the results of the Spanish Mission Program? Was it a success? Did they accomplish what they set out to do? Was it even a doable project or beyond the capabilities of the times?

2. What are the unique aspects of life today in the State of Texas that can be connected to the Spanish Mission Program? How has our current culture been enriched by the existence of the Mission experience in our history?

Answers to Study Questions for Part Four

1. 1598, Juan de Oñate
2. 1610, Santa Fe, New Mexico
3. 1629, 1632, Father Juan de Salas
4. Santa Fe, New Mexico, Jumano Indians, San Angelo
5. Evangelization of Native Americans
6. Caddoan and Hasinain Native American, friend or ally, "Hello Friend"
7. San Antonio de Valero, 1718
8. 1682
9. Fort Saint Louis, La Salle, 1684
10. Mature in Roman Catholic Christianity, learn the Spanish language, understand Spanish political and economic matters and learn vocational skills.

Study Questions for Part Five

1. There were three main groups of settlers in the Texas territory prior to the arrival of the Anglo-Protestants from America: the Native Americans, the Spanish and the _____ ___.

2. What was the main non-religious factor that began bringing American Protestants into Texas starting in 1820 despite the danger of hostile Indians?

3. The Protestant Reformation started in the year _____ as a result of the protest of one particular member of the Catholic clergy whose name was _____ ___.

4. In 1382 against the wishes of the Catholic Church, _____ became the first person to translate the entire Bible into English.

5. What are the names of the first five Protestant colonies in America and in what years were they established?

6. What is the name of the first Protestant preacher to come into Texas, what church Denomination did he represent and where did he establish the first Protestant church in the Texas territory?

7. What is the name of the oldest continuously operating Baptist church in Texas, where is it located and what is the name of the famous person who was baptized there?

8. In what year did the first Sunday School in Texas start, what was the name of the preacher who started it, what Denomination did he represent and where did it start?

9. In 1832 there was a church meeting in Sabine County conducted in part by a famous Presbyterian pistol-toting minister named _____. The illegal meeting was reported to the Mexican authorities and the commander of the local garrison in Nacogdoches by the name of _____ made the following statement recorded in Texas history for all time: *Are they stealing anything? Are they killing anybody? Are they doing anything bad?"* And because the answer to all his questions was "No" he allowed the meeting to continue.

10. In what year was the Spanish land grant program initiated and what did the new Mexican government do about it in 1821 when they won their independence?

11. Name the five uncommon hero settlers in the forgoing section that have had such a great impact on Texas history.

12. Which of the uncommon settlers is known as the Father of Texas?

13. Which of the uncommon settlers was in command at the Alamo?

14. Which of the uncommon settlers came to Texas as an experienced and successful politician?

15. Which of the uncommon settlers married the daughter of the mayor of San Antonio?

16. Which of the uncommon settlers has been called the George Washington of Texas and has a major Texas city named after him?

Discussion Questions for Part Five

1. How did the First Great Awakening prepare the people who only 65 years later would become settlers in the Mexican territory of Texas?

2. How is it possible that five men with such difficulty in each of their past lives could have so changed their ways of thinking and acting to become special heroes in Texas history?

3. How would you have responded to the requirements of becoming a Texas settler back in 1825: no airplanes or cars for transportation, no cell phones, no televisions, no electricity, no ice, plenty of hostile not very receptive Native Americans, no roads, no cities for hundreds of miles, no super markets, no plumbing, no A/C, etc?

Answers to Study Questions for Part Five

1. Mexicans
2. Spanish and Mexican land-grant programs
3. 1517, Martin Luther
4. John Wycliffe
5. Saint Augustine (1565), Roanoke (1584), Jamestown (1607), Plymouth (1620), Massachusetts Bay (1628)
6. William Stephenson, Methodist, Jonesborough in present-day Red River County

7. Independence Baptist Church, Independence, Texas, Sam Houston
8. 1829, T. J. Pilgrim, Baptist, San Felipe
9. Sumner Bacon, Col. José Piedras
10. 1820, they continued it
11. Stephen F. Austin, Sam Houston, Col. William Travis, David Crockett and James Bowie
12. Stephen F. Austin
13. Col. William Travis
14. David Crockett
15. James Bowie
16. Sam Houston

Study Questions for Part Six

1. On March 2, 1836 a new country was formed called the Republic of Texas. How many people signed the Texas Declaration of Independence and where was it signed?

2. What was the name of the Political Party that had been the most vocal and influential in the general agitation for independence that arose after 1830?

3. What happened in 1830 that caused the relationship between Texas and Mexico to reach a low point that eventually led to revolution?

4. Who was the leader of the committee selected by the constitutional convention to draft a Texas Declaration of Independence and what was the name of that constitutional convention?

5. Name the six principle reasons listed in this article that were given for declaring independence from Mexico.

6. Which complaint number of the *Texas Declaration of Independence* dealt with the subject of religious freedom?

7. What was the name of the commanding officer of the Texicans at the battle of the Alamo and what were the names of three principal Texas heroes who died there when the Alamo was overrun by the Mexican Army on the date of _____?

8. What was the name of the battle that defeated the Mexican army and established a new country, who was the commanding officer of the Texican Army and what was the date of the victory?

9. What was the name of the first Baptist missionaries coming into Texas?

10. Who was elected the first president of the Republic of Texas?

Discussion Question for Part Six

Consider that in one form or another the three heroes William Travis, David Crockett and James Bowie resisted the authority of Sam Houston and wound up dying in the Alamo. What if they had obeyed General Houston's orders, abandoned the Alamo and joined his army? Did disobedience produce their heroism or would they have been heroic anyway?

Answers to Study Questions for Part Six

1. 60, Washington on the Brazos
2. The War Party
3. Further emigration of settlers from the US was stopped by the Mexican government
4. George Childress, Convention of 1836
5. Mexico had become a military dictatorship, the Mexican government had reneged on their promises of constitutional liberty and a republican government, the Texas territory was too far away from its capital city of Saltillo, basic political rights were denied like the right to keep and bear arms bear arms and trial by jury, there was no system of public education, no freedom of religion
6. Complaint #16
7. Col. William Travis was the commanding officer, David Crockett and James Bowie were the two heroes who joined Travis in death and the Alamo was defeated on March 6, 1836.
8. The Battle of San Jacinto, General Sam Houston, April 21, 1836
9. James Huckins
10. Sam Houston

Study Questions for Part Seven

1. On what date did the Republic of Texas finally accept the invitation from the United States to become the twenty-eighth state in the Union?

2. Which American President led the political fight for the annexation of Texas at the expense of his own career and what was the name of the President who succeeded him and signed the invitation to Texas for annexation?

3. What was the name of the main presidential candidate who ran against James K. Polk and John Tyler in 1844 and what was the name of his political party?

4. What was the name of the last President of the Republic of Texas before it became a state in the union at the end of 1845?

5. What was the name of the first governor of the State of Texas when it became a state in the union at the end of 1845?

6. On what date did the United States declare war against Mexico?

7. On what date were negotiations completed for a treaty between the U.S. and Mexico and what was the name given to the Treaty?

8. Can you name the seven present-day states of the U.S. covered by the Treaty that ended the Mexican-American war? How much did the U.S. agree to pay for this new territory despite the fact that Mexico had been defeated in the war?

9. Name the two generals in the U.S. Army who became heroes because of their victories in the Mexican American War: the first became President of the U.S. and the second was the longest serving General in the history of the U. S.

10. Each General is famous for their two particular victories during the Mexican-American War that are mentioned in this book. Name the battles (a total of four) and associate them with each General.

11. In 1861 the Governor of Texas refused to submit himself to the Confederacy and was subsequently removed from office by the State Legislature. Name that governor.

12. What was the primary role and function of the State of Texas during the Civil War?

13. Name the General who was the Commander of the Texas Brigade in Northern Virginia.

14. Name the highest ranking *Tejano* to serve in the Confederate military.

15. What was the name of the President who replaced Abraham Lincoln and presided over the first phase of post–was Reconstruction?

16. In what year was Texas readmitted to the Union? And in what year did Reconstruction end?

17. Historians are in general agreement that the Church in Texas did a particularly effective job of providing societal services in two necessary endeavors. Name the two areas.

18. Name the two oldest universities in the State of Texas and the Christian denomination that each is affiliated with.

19. What was the name of the first Baptist newspaper in Texas and who founded it?

20. The man who founded the first Baptist newspaper was an ancestor of a famous man. Who was famous descendent and why is he famous?

Discussion Questions for Part Seven

1. Many people feel that Mexico wasn't treated fairly during and after the Mexican–American War and that people of Mexican descent now living in Texas should be able to fly their Mexican flag above the American flag and claim their affiliation with Mexico instead of the U.S. How do you feel about this issue of political correctness?

2. Do you feel that the American Civil War was primarily about slavery or states' rights, and why?

3. Why did it take Texas so long to get through Reconstruction and to finally be readmitted to the Union?

Answers to Study Questions for Part Seven

1. December 29, 1845
2. President John Tyler, President James K. Polk
3. Henry Clay, Whig Party
4. Anson Jones
5. James Pinckney Henderson
6. May 13, 1846
7. February 2, 1848, *Treaty of Guadelupe Hidalgo*
8. New Mexico, Utah, Nevada, Arizona, California, Texas, and Colorado; 15 million dollars + up to 3.5 million dollars for claims of U.S. citizens against the Mexican government.
9. Zachary Taylor, Winfield Scott
10. General Taylor: Monterrey and Buena Vista; General Winfield Scott: Vera Cruz and Mexico City
11. Sam Houston
12. Western breadbasket of the Confederacy
13. General John Bell Hood
14. Col. Santos Benavides
15. Andrew Johnson
16. 1870, 1874
17. Education, Newspapers
18. Southwestern University–Methodist, Baylor University–Baptist
19. The Texas Baptist, George Washington Baines
20. Lyndon Baines Johnson, thirty-sixth president of the United States

Study Questions for Part Eight

1. Where did the cattle in Texas come from and about when did they start arriving?

2. The two main groups of Texas cattlemen have always been the _____ and the_____.

3. The difference between a ranch and a farm is that a ranch is a place where _____ is produced and a farm is where _____ are produced.

4. The Spanish word for cowboy is _____.

5. The entire idea of herding livestock from horseback came from _____ tradition with clear roots all the way back to ancient _____.

6. When did the Mexican-Vaquero culture give way to the new American-Cowboy culture?

7. The name of the most famous Cattle Trail was the _____ _____.

8. What were the names of the other three famous cattle trails?

9. What was the name of the trail that eventually replaced the Chisholm Trail?

10. What is Joseph Farwell Glidden known for and where was he from? How did what he is known for change the Cattle Industry forever.

Discussion Questions for Part Eight

1. How did the Texas cattle industry directly influence the expansion of Christianity over the years?

2. Try imagining yourself as a Christian living at various times over the five hundred year history of the cattle industry in Texas. How would you have pursued your faith in those times? As a settler in 1821? Living on a ranch just after the Mexican-American War in 1849? Working on a cattle drive on the Chisholm Trail in 1866? Living in a new town that depended on revenue from the cattle drives?

Answers to Study Questions for Part Eight

1. From Mexico by early cattle drives in the 1540's
3. Ranchers, cowboys
4. Livestock, crops
5. Vaquero
6. During the Mexican-American War 1846-1848
7. Arabic, Persia
8. Chisholm Trail
9. Shawnee Trail. Goodnight-Loving Trail, Western Trail
10. The Western Trail
11. Invented barbed wire, Illinois; closed the Cattle Trails and shifted transportation to the railroads

Study Questions for Part Nine

1. The word prosperity is mentioned in Scripture almost _____ times.

2. The first European to encounter crude oil in Texas was _____ and what purpose did he use it for?

3. The first process to distill kerosene from crude oil was invented by _____ who was from _____.

4. The first commercial oil well drilled in the U.S. was drilled in Pennsylvania. Who drilled it and in what year?

5. In what year and where was the first producing oil well in Texas drilled?

6. Where was the first economically significant oil discovery in Texas and in what year was the first well drilled? Who drilled it and what famous oil company did he help found later?

7. The oil discovery that jump started the Texas transformation into a major oil producer was the famous _____ oil field.

8. What are the three major kinds of fossil fuels?

9. How do we know that it was God who initiated the presence of fossil fuels?

10. What is the big advantage of fossil fuels versus all of the various alternative fuels?

Discussion Questions for Part Nine

1. Why do some people see as curses what are actually blessings from God?

2. Some people say that the earth is deteriorating because of sin. Give some examples of the curse working on the earth.

3. Do you believe that fossil fuels are harming the planet? And if you do believe it, can you cite some credible sources of information to substantiate it?

Answers to Study Questions for Part Nine

1. 100
2. Luis de Moscosso, to caulk his leaking boats
3. Abraham Gesner, Nova Scotia, Canada
4. Edwin Drake, 1859
5. 1866, Nacogdoches County
6. Corsicana, 1894, Joseph Cullinan, Texaco
7. Spindletop
8. Oil, Natural Gas, Coal
9. Because God initiated the flood knowing that in the aftermath fossil fuels would be formed
10. Less expensive

Discussion Questions for Part Ten

Learning the answers to the following questions will change your life and provide a strong foundation for you to become a strong and victorious Christian:

1. What does the Scripture mean when it says that God has decided to not remember our sins? (See Hebrews 8:12 and 10:17)

2. What does the Scripture mean when it says that God is not holding us accountable for our sins? (See 2 Corinthians 5:19, Romans 4:8, 4:15, and 5:13)

3. What does the Scripture mean when it says that Jesus has ALREADY paid for the sins of all mankind for all time? (See 1 John 2:2, 1 Timothy 4:10, 2:4-6, Titus 2:11, Romans 5:18-19, Hebrews 2:9, 10:12, 9:12)

Virtual Bibliography

Almost all of the research behind the foregoing articles was carried out on the Internet. A lot of *Part Ten* came straight out of my Bible. To find what I studied, just paste the following Internet addresses into your browser to obtain the same information I used to write the articles. There is a wealth of information on the Internet about the history of Texas and I have scarcely scratched the surface of it for this particularly specialized subject. If you like history, Texas has a wonderfully rich history to be pursued and loved!

http://creation.com/how-old-is-the-earth
http://en.wikipedia.org/wiki/Human_evolution
http://christiananswers.net/q-aig/**garden**-of-**eden**-loc.html
https://answersingenesis.org/tower-of-babel/native-americans-and-the-bible/
http://www.orthodox.cn/localchurch/200406ancientcnhist_en.htm
http://creationwiki.org/Tower_of_Babel
http://en.wikipedia.org/wiki/Indigenous_peoples_of_the_Americas
http://www.creationworldview.org/articles.asp
Why Do Men Believe Evolution Against All Odds, book by Dr. Carl E. Baugh, Bible Belt Publishing, Bethany, Oklahoma
http://news.nationalgeographic.com/news/2013/11/131120-science-native-american-people-migration-siberia-genetics/
http://www.glencoe.com/sec/socialstudies/btt/columbus/before_the_voyage.shtml
http://en.wikipedia.org/wiki/Moors
http://en.wikipedia.org/wiki/Christopher_Columbus
http://en.wikipedia.org/wiki/Luis_de_Moscoso_Alvarado
http://en.wikipedia.org/wiki/John_Wycliffe
http://en.wikipedia.org/wiki/Gutenberg_Bible
http://www.aloha.net/~mikesch/banned.htm
http://celebratingtexas.com
http://www.aztec-history.com/hernan-cortez-biography.html
http://www.pbs.org/kpbs/theborder/history/timeline/1.html
http://www.lsjunction.com/events/events.htm
http://campus.kellerisd.net/Teachers/11948/Homework%20Review/Chapter%205.1.pdf
http://en.wikipedia.org/wiki/Six_flags_over_Texas
http://campus.kellerisd.net/Teachers/11948/Homework%20Review/Chapter%205.3.pdf
http://www.texasalmanac.com/topics/history/religion-early-texas
https://www.tshaonline.org/
http://en.wikipedia.org/wiki/Spanish_missions_in_the_Americas
http://www.tshaonline.org/handbook/online/articles/pft04
http://en.wikipedia.org/wiki/Spanish_missions_in_Texas#Mission_San_Francisco_de_la_Espada
http://www.h-net.org/~latam/powerpoints/spanishmissionsoftexas.pdf
http://www.tamu.edu/faculty/ccbn/dewitt/adp/history/mission_period/valero/missionlife.html
http://www.let.rug.nl/usa/essays/1801-1900/anglo-american-colonization-in-texas/texas-1821-1836.php
http://www.let.rug.nl/usa/essays/1801-1900/anglo-american-colonization-in-texas/texas-1836-1848.php
https://www.tshaonline.org/handbook/online/articles/uma01
http://en.wikipedia.org/wiki/Jean_Lafitte
http://en.wikipedia.org/wiki/Church_of_England
http://en.wikipedia.org/wiki/Roanoke_Colony
http://en.wikipedia.org/wiki/Jamestown,_Virginia

http://en.wikipedia.org/wiki/Plymouth_Colony
http://en.wikipedia.org/wiki/Massachusetts_Bay_Colony
http://en.wikipedia.org/wiki/First_Great_Awakening
http://en.wikipedia.org/wiki/Stephen_F._Austin
http://americanhistory.about.com/od/colonialamerica/p/great_awakening.htm
http://en.wikipedia.org/wiki/History_of_Protestantism_in_the_United_States
http://www.cemetery.state.tx.us/pub/user_form.asp?pers_id=3
http://www.biography.com/people/sam-houston-9344806
http://www.tamu.edu/faculty/ccbn/dewitt/adp/history/bios/crockett/crockett.html
http://latinamericanhistory.about.com/od/TexasIndependence/p/Biography-Of-Jim-Bowie.htm
http://www.independencetx.com/IndependenceBaptistChurch.htm
http://www.tamu.edu/faculty/ccbn/dewitt/adp/history/bios/travis/travis.html
http://www.biography.com/people/sam-houston-9344806
http://en.wikipedia.org/wiki/Davy_Crockett
http://en.wikipedia.org/wiki/James_Bowie
http://en.wikipedia.org/wiki/Law_of_April_6,_1830
http://en.wikipedia.org/wiki/Texas_Declaration_of_Independence
http://en.wikipedia.org/wiki/Battle_of_the_Alamo
http://en.wikipedia.org/wiki/Texas_in_the_American_Civil_War
http://en.wikipedia.org/wiki/History_of_Texas_%281845%E2%80%9360%29
http://www.pbs.org/wgbh/amex/reconstruction/states/sf_timeline.html
http://wiki.answers.com/Q/What_year_did_the_former_confederate_states_rejoin_the_union?#slide=1
http://en.wikipedia.org/wiki/Conclusion_of_the_American_Civil_War
http://texasindependencetrail.com/plan-your-adventure/historic-sites-and-cities/sites/independence-baptist-church-and-texas-baptist#sthash.n6hQOVGR.dpuf
http://www.tamu.edu/faculty/ccbn/dewitt/allgrantmap.htm
http://clmroots.blogspot.com/2012/04/john-sadler-true-texan.html
http://www.humanitiestexas.org/news/events/signers-texas-declaration-independence-6
http://drtlibrary.wordpress.com/2009/03/11/newspaper-accounts-of-the-battle-of-the-alamo/
http://sites.allegheny.edu/about/history/presidents/martin-ruter/
http://en.wikipedia.org/wiki/Texas_annexation
http://www.shmoop.com/manifest-destiny-mexican-american-war/henry-clay.html
http://www.britannica.com/EBchecked/topic/379134/Mexican-American-War
http://www.dmwv.org/mexwar/mwart/prints.htm
http://www.britannica.com/EBchecked/topic/379134/Mexican-American-War
http://www.sonofthesouth.net/texas/flags-republic-texas.htm
http://en.wikipedia.org/wiki/Zachary_Taylor
http://en.wikipedia.org/wiki/File:Antonio_Lopez_de_Santa_Anna_c1853.png
http://en.wikipedia.org/wiki/Winfield_Scott
http://www.damasocanales.com/vintage/general-taylor-at-monterrey-zachary-taylor-on-horseback-monterrey-mexico-engraving/
http://www.tamu.edu/faculty/ccbn/dewitt/innerresidents3o-z2.htm
http://www.cleburnetimesreview.com/features/x563625290/Mike-Beard-Sumner-Bacon-s-mission-in-Texas-endures
http://www.tshaonline.org/handbook/online/articles/imu01
To Survive and Excel, book by William B. Jones, Southwestern University, First Edition 2006
http://www.texashistory.com/Store/tabid/145/CategoryID/1/List/0/Level/1/ProductID/5/Language/en-US/Default.aspx?SortField=ProductName%2CProductName
http://celticcowboy.com/19THTX.htm
http://www.cumberland.org/hfcpc/minister/BaconS.htm
http://en.wikipedia.org/wiki/Six_flags_over_Texas

McGill Traveling Papers courtesy of John S. Miller family archives, Puluxy, Texas

http://en.wikipedia.org/wiki/Texas_in_the_American_Civil_War

www.tamut.edu/.../TX/Civil%20War

http://texasourtexas.texaspbs.org/the-eras-of-texas/civil-war-reconstruction/

http://en.wikipedia.org/wiki/James_W._Throckmorton

http://en.wikipedia.org/wiki/Elisha_M._Pease

http://en.wikipedia.org/wiki/Edmund_J._Davis

http://www.ushistory.org/us/22c.asp

http://en.wikipedia.org/wiki/Christian_revival

Holy Bible, Updated NAS, Foundation Publications, copyright 1960 by Lockman Foundation

http://en.wikipedia.org/wiki/Compromise_of_1850

http://www.tshaonline.org/handbook/online/articles/cfs01

http://www.sjsu.edu/faculty/watkins/cowboyculture.htm

http://www.texasbeyondhistory.net/st-plains/images/he14.html

https://www.tshaonline.org/handbook/online/articles/azr02

https://www.tshaonline.org/handbook/online/articles/ayc01

http://www.texasalmanac.com/topics/agriculture/cattle-drives-started-earnest-after-civil-war

http://www.thelonghornalliance.com/default.asp?contentID=%20579

http://www.statesymbolsusa.org/Lists/state_mammals.html

http://en.wikipedia.org/wiki/Cattle_drives_in_the_United_States

http://news.nationalgeographic.com/news/2003/08/0814_030815_cowboys_2.html

http://en.wikipedia.org/wiki/Vaquero

http://en.wikipedia.org/wiki/Treaty_of_Paris_%281763%29

http://www.history.com/topics/louisiana-purchase

http://sefarad.org/sefarad/sefarad.php/id/13/

http://www.encyclopedia.com/topic/Cattle_drives.aspx

http://www.birdseyeviews.org/teaching-resources/tr-middle-02-a.pdf

http://www.theshawneetrail.com/

http://www.tshaonline.org/handbook/online/articles/ayw02

http://www.texasalmanac.com/topics/business/oil-and-texas-cultural-history

http://en.wikipedia.org/wiki/Texas_Oil_Boom

http://www.tshaonline.org/handbook/online/articles/doogz

http://www.texasescapes.com/DEPARTMENTS/Guest_Columnists/East_Texas_all_things_historical/LyneTaliaferroBarret1AMD201.htm

http://en.wikipedia.org/wiki/Nouveau_riche

https://search.yahoo.com/yhs/search?p=abraham+gesner+biography&ei=UTF8&hspart=mozilla&hsimp=yhs-001

http://priweb.org/ed/pgws/history/pennsylvania/pennsylvania.html

http://en.wikipedia.org/wiki/Instrumental_temperature_record

ABOUT THE AUTHOR

Dr. Bill Miller is an ordained cross-denominational minister, elder and the founder of a national nonprofit Christian organization called *Make A Way Ministries.* He has been involved in financial counseling and teaching since 1985 and has assisted tens of thousands of families to overcome financial problems and get on to financial success and victory.

He also pastored the bilingual (English/Spanish) *Faith Life Fellowship Church* in Miami Florida from 2007 until mid-2012.

Dr. Miller has published a bible-based financial e-newsletter called *Prosperous Life Newsletter* since January 1998 and has written more than 25 books about various financial topics with the purpose of helping families overcome financial problems on a practical level.

This publication connecting Texas history and Christianity is his first effort outside the financial arena and he has promised that it will not be his last.

Dr. Bill was born in Houston, Texas a long time ago and is a graduate of *Texas Tech University* in Lubbock. He also holds a Doctorate in Ministry from *Miami Christian University.*

He currently lives happily and works busily with his wife Sherri in the historic community of Granbury, Texas.